July 1995

To Berman

Happy Birthday

With Byrd
at the Bottom
of the World

The South Pole Expedition of 1928–1930

Dream Big and Dare to Fail

Norman D. Vaughan
with Cecil B. Murphey

Norman D. Vaughan.

Stackpole Books

Published by
STACKPOLE BOOKS
Cameron and Kelker Streets
P.O. Box 1831
Harrisburg PA 17105

Printed in the United States of America

First Edition

10 9 8 7

Maps by Sarah Mittelstadt Bean

Grateful acknowledgment is made for permission to reprint excerpts from the
following works:

Little America © 1930 by Richard E. Byrd, published by G.P. Putnam's Sons.
Used with the permission of Richard E. Byrd, III.

Cold © 1931 by Laurence M. Gould, published by Carleton College. Used with
the permission of the author.

South of the Sun © 1934 by Russell Owen, published by John Day. Used with
the permission of Harper & Row Inc., 10 East 53rd Street, New York, NY
10022.

Library of Congress Cataloging-in-Publication Data

Vaughan, Norman D.
　　With Byrd at the bottom of the world / Norman D. Vaughan with
　Cecil Murphey. — 1st ed.
　　　　p.　cm.
　　ISBN 0-8117-1904-9
　　1. Byrd Antarctic Expedition (1st: 1928–1930)　I. Murphey, Cecil.
　II. Title.
　G850 1928.V38
　919.8904 — dc20　　　　　　　　　　　　　　　　89-26182

CONTENTS

FOREWORD

Col. Norman Vaughan has crammed enough high adventure into his mere eighty-four years to sap the adrenalin of a battalion of lifetimes. What's more, he's still doing it.

As I write this, he's in Greenland, engaged in salvaging two B-17s and six P-38s, which crashed in 1942. Just prior to that he drove dogs for the twelfth time over Alaska's grueling 1,158-mile Iditarod Trail. As perhaps might be expected, his elapsed time hardly challenged that of the winner. After all, the colonel, ever a gentleman, would be loath to barge rudely ahead of a young woman, his junior by half a century.

Though it's been forty years since I ran dogs on a high-country trapline along the Iditarod, I can well recall the challenge of doing so and find it incredible that someone almost old enough to be my father could have made it to the first race checkpoint, much less to Front Street in Nome.

Not that I'm not pretty rugged myself. For example, when I was a kid I could beat most men twice my age at wrist wrestling. And by George, you know, I still can. But I wouldn't want to challenge the colonel. No siree. Whether we're talking sinew or spirit, Norman Vaughan is second to no one.

He and I have too seldom crossed trails, but each time we have done so, I've gleaned nuggets of imagination, incentive, and inspiration: gifts that enliven this book, about an epic antarctic adventure he had back when I was a stripling. For his enduring generosity and zest for life I am both grateful and envious. In fact, when I finally grow up, I hope I'm just like him.

GOVERNOR JAY S. HAMMOND
Port Alsworth, Alaska

FOREWORD

Inveterate adventurer Norman Vaughan first came bounding into my life in 1986. En route to Alaska for his eighth running of Alaska's eleven-hundred-mile Iditarod sled dog race — quite deservedly called the Last Great Race on Earth — he stopped by my home to extend congratulations to my expedition colleague, Will Steger, and me for our successful dog sled journey to the North Pole.

Spotting an account of Admiral Richard Byrd's 1929 flight to the South Pole on my bookshelf, he pulled it down and excitedly flipped to the photo section. There he found what he was looking for. It was a playful scene of expedition team members entertaining each other with a vaudeville act during the long night of the Antarctic winter at their Little America base camp.

"That's me!" he beamed, pointing to an athletic figure who sported a coating of greasepaint and an impish grin. The countenance of the young man, then twenty-five years old, matched perfectly that of its current owner, now an octogenarian.

The intervening years had thinned his curly mop of dark hair to a white crown and etched his robust smile, but it was clear to me that Vaughan brimmed with an infectious exuberance that had never waned.

"I'm still hoping to get back down there, maybe even reach the pole by dog sled," he said. "But that may have to wait a few years. You see, we're busy with a project in Greenland right now. We're launching an expedition to locate and retrieve a plane that was abandoned there in World War II and is now buried under a few hundred feet of glacial ice."

The Iditarod beckoned first, so he was off with his sled dogs to Alaska. Over the next few years I tracked his progress as he entered more Iditarod races and located that buried airplane. And if he hasn't yet reached the South Pole, it isn't for want of trying. Thus I knew that upon receiving the manuscript for this book, I would be reading no pompous resting-on-my-laurels record of a man's youthful shot at glory. Rather, this book is a recounting that is fresh and crisp. Rarely does one find an adventure book that is as seasoned and tempered by the reflections of a lifetime and yet reads with the forthrightness and immediacy of a diary.

The 1928–1930 expedition members were contractually bound by Byrd not to publish anything for at least one year after the expedition. "I waited sixty," Vaughan says dryly, and we can be glad he did. What we read is a thoughtful distillation of his most gripping experiences and the most poignant moments of his association with Byrd both on and off the ice.

Among the significant contributions this book makes to the growing library of expedition literature is the portrait it paints of the personal qualities that destine someone to spend a lifetime pursuing adventure. A willingness to take risks and a fascination with the unknown certainly rank high among these, but from Vaughan's account it's clear that jaunty determination should also be on the list.

His book opens with an example of just such a quality: how, as a relatively inexperienced twenty-two-year-old, Vaughan talked his way onto the expedition roster. Using a strategy that he seems to have employed throughout his life, he refused to accept rejection: when a door is slammed in your face, he writes, you just enter through a different door.

The adventure, like Vaughan, bounds along from there through the months of expedition preparations, to a winter spent on the ice cap, to the climax: a fifteen-hundred-mile, eighty-seven-day journey by dog sled, traversing a quarter of the continent. This epic trek positioned Vaughan and five teammates to rescue Byrd if he had to land his plane. The stories Vaughan tells along the way rank among the best found in any expedition book.

A reader doesn't need to be a fanatic dog musher, as I am, to be captivated by the dog stories in this volume. Animal lovers should be forewarned, however. Modern readers with modern sensibilities will enter an era when the realities of expedition logistics were considerably harsher than they are today. At a time when resupply by aircraft was not possible, the accepted and essential practice was to feed weaker dogs to strong dogs as an expedition progressed. Vaughan recalls the emotional anguish he faced when he found himself obliged to dispatch dogs he had raised and trained and grown attached to—most memorably a very special dog named Belle.

The glimpses one gets of Richard Byrd throughout the book maintains the enigma of an explorer who managed his ambitions and notoriety with quiet dignity. Vaughan's admiration and gratitude toward him are expressed in enthusiastic, but not fawning, terms; ultimately, Vaughan discovers that his hero is prone to the same human foibles as anyone else.

One of the beauties of this book is that it frames the expedition in the context of Vaughan's entire life to date. The closing chapters include his bittersweet reflections on his efforts to reconcile family life with his insatiable quest for adventure. Many of us who weave adventure throughout our lives share this dilemma, and Vaughan's honest accounting offers consolation.

During the question-and-answer sessions that follow the talks I give about my expeditions, someone inevitably asks, "Why are you driven to subject yourself to the rigors and risks of expeditions in polar regions?" Vaughan's book sheds light on the answer in ways that are understandable even to those who are least passionate about adventure. For Vaughan's adventure story—his life, in fact—makes it clear that the spirit of adventure is not just a youthful fling or a headlong thrust for fame and fortune. Rather, it's an innate human quality that blossoms and flourishes in certain people and becomes a guiding influence throughout their lives—even as they approach their ninetieth year.

PAUL SCHURKE
Ely, Minnesota

To the memory of
Edward E. Goodale,
Frederick F. Crockett,
and John R. Bird,
who went with me to Antarctica,
and to the one man we all loved,
Dr. Laurence McKinley Gould,
second in command of the Byrd Antarctic Expedition 1928–1930,
who is affectionately known as Mr. Antarctica;

to my two children,
Gerard Gould
and Jacqueline Lee,
who had frustrating lives bringing up their father;

and lastly to my wife Carolyn,
who struggled to help me finish this book
and is the strongest supporter
of my continuing adventuresome life

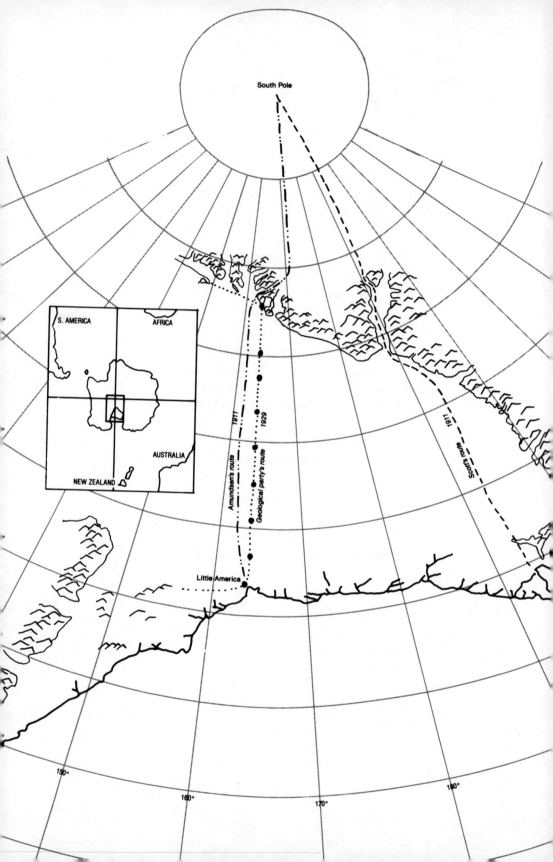

Prologue

With only the slightest hesitation, I approached the house at 9 Brimmer Street. It was a typical five-story building in the Back Bay, *the* residential section for Bostonians. The rear of the house, with a balcony on each floor, overlooked the Charles River Basin with its popular esplanade, a forty-foot-wide concrete walk with a high protective railing.

After ringing the bell, I nervously shifted my weight from one foot to the other. I hardly noticed the unusual warmth of the September morning in 1927 as I rehearsed what I would say to the commander. My first words had to get me inside.

A few seconds passed, and getting no response, I rang a second time. Through the frosted glass I could see a small entryway and a second door into the house proper. The inside door opened and closed and a shadowy figure moved toward me. The outside door opened to reveal a tall woman with a commanding presence. She wore a simple uniform-dress. I guessed her to be about fifty. She didn't say a word, just stared down at me and scowled.

"Is Commander Byrd at home?" I asked.

"Yes."

"May I see him?"

"Not unless you have an appointment." The officiousness in her voice made her attitude clear. "Do you have an appointment?"

"No," I said, "I don't, but—"

"Then you can't see him."

"It's quite important." Not willing to give up so easily, I added, "I must see him!"

She leaned toward me. "Nobody gets by me without an appointment."

"If he would see me for ten minutes. Just five—"

She folded her large arms across her ample breasts. "I said, nobody gets by me without an appointment."

It had not occurred to me that I wouldn't be allowed to see Byrd. I turned and walked slowly down the steps to the street, dazed by the rejection.

My whole life seemed to fall down the steps with me. I mumbled to myself: *My chance of a lifetime is gone. I can't get in to see the commander. If I can't get in to see him, I'll never be able to go.* The more I thought of what had just happened, the more depressed I became. I had never felt so dejected.

I was trying to think what else I might do with my life when suddenly an idea burst into my consciousness. The maid had slammed the door in my face; instead of figuring how to get past her, I would enter through a different door. And this time, my plan would work.

Magic Words

Only moments before, I had walked down Brimmer Street, totally downcast. My stride picked up and I half ran for more than a mile. Each step built up my sagging morale. Until I reached the *Boston Transcript* building, I didn't pause. Once there, I walked casually inside, filled with an air of confidence.

My plan was to meet W. A. McDonald, a longtime reporter and highly respected journalist who had written several articles about Byrd and obviously knew the famous naval commander well. I would ask him to speak with Byrd on my behalf. Although I had never met the newsman, surely he would be delighted to function as my appointment maker.

I asked for the reporter at the desk, prepared to argue if anyone tried to stop me. To my surprise, the man sent me straight to the editorial department. When I reached the right floor, someone pointed out McDonald's desk.

I looked him over as I approached. He was short, in his midforties, with salt-and-pepper hair; the first aging lines had etched themselves across the contours of his face. He wore glasses so thick I couldn't see the color of his eyes. He sat behind a large desk heaped with stacks of newspapers. Next to the papers rested a telephone, a typewriter, and a pad of paper, leaving him a small area for work.

I introduced myself and said, "I read your fine story about Commander Byrd, and I want to go on the expedition."

He leaned back in his chair and stared at me, his face devoid of any expression. "Why come to me? I don't have anything to do with the expedition."

"I realize that, Mr. McDonald," I replied confidently, having already prepared myself for his answer. "But you know him. Besides, I've already been to his house and I couldn't get in to see him. I want to go on that expedition. I've got to go!"

"That so?" Despite his noncommittal answer, I detected a spark of interest.

"Yes, sir. And I'll do anything to get that chance."

"I see," he said. "And what qualifications do you have?" His face took on a sternness.

I hesitated, wondering if I would have to fight the same hostile protectiveness that the maid had shown. I could almost hear him say, "You're nothing but a stranger, riffraff, just a youngster. You're not going to get by *me*."

This time I was not going to give up; McDonald was going to intercede for me. I inhaled deeply and said, "I'm a dog driver and I've had a lot of experience."

"Is that so?"

"Yes, it is. I spent the winter of 1925 driving dogs for Doctor Grenfell."

"You mean Doctor Wilfred Grenfell? Tell me about that."

I told him I had dropped out of Harvard two years earlier to work with the much-admired Sir Wilfred Grenfell. A successful British physician, Grenfell left England in 1892 and had been serving ever since as a medical missionary to the Eskimos in Labrador and Newfoundland. He traveled the coastal waters in a specially equipped hospital ship and went overland by dog sled. For eight months I drove his dog sled in Labrador and observed a dedicated humanitarian ministering to the health and educational needs of the fishermen of the region, winning their respect and international recognition for his unceasing devotion to their welfare. He had established schools, hospitals, nursing centers, stores, even industrial projects in that barren land.

"You actually worked with the dogs?"

"I certainly did," I said. "And I still do. When I finished my work with Grenfell, I brought back my own dog, Storm, along with two others. My friend Eddie Goodale has a dog, and so does my father. I could have five dogs available for the expedition."

"So you're a dog musher, huh?" He leaned forward, making me feel I was undergoing a police interrogation. "Where do you drive dogs? This part of the country isn't like Labrador."

"I do it right here in New England all the time." I explained that I belonged to the New England Sled Dog Club, which fostered the breeding, training, and racing of sled dogs.

"I've heard of the club over the wires," he said, "but I don't know much about it."

Ever the reporter, eliciting facts, he gave me the opportunity to talk about one of my favorite topics. I told him far more about dogs and the sled dog club than he probably wanted to hear. But he continued to listen. Since there was still a chance that he'd refuse to make contact for me, I kept talking lest he turn me down.

Although occasionally interrupting with questions, he listened intently. The stern expression drained from his face, and he relaxed. Encouraged now that he might do what he could for me, I said, "And while reading your article in yesterday's *Transcript*, I felt I had to go on the expedition."

"Oh? Feel that strong, huh?" he said, the first hint of a smile on his face.

The evening before had decided it. Five of us were studying at a table in a Harvard dormitory. Hearing the outside door open, I glanced up, always ready for a disruption from my books. The other four, deeply involved with their assignments, paid no attention to the paperboy who tossed me the *Boston Transcript*.

I unfolded the paper, intending to read only the headlines before resuming my studies. In large, bold letters I read five magic words that would change the direction of my life: BYRD TO THE SOUTH POLE.

"Listen to this!" I dropped the paper on the table and pointed to the headline. "He's going to do it! Byrd's going to the Pole!" My eyes hurried down the two columns, and I turned the page. The already-famous U.S. navy commander, Richard Evelyn Byrd, was going to fly over the South Pole — a feat never before attempted.

Like most Americans, I had been avidly following the career of Byrd, who had emerged as one of the world's great explorers alongside Robert Scott, Robert Edwin Peary, and Roald Amundsen.

Like them, he was determined to conquer the North and South poles. Since the turn of the century, the exploration of the two polar regions had captured the attention of the whole world. These events were taking place in my lifetime, and I had read voraciously about the men and their achievements, often picturing myself traveling with these pioneers.

An American, Robert Peary, had reached the North Pole by dog team in 1911. In that same year Roald Amundsen, a Norwegian, had planned to reach the North Pole. On learning that Peary had already started north, he secretly headed his crew southward to compete with a British naval officer, Lieutenant Robert F. Scott, who was attempting to discover the geographic South Pole.

When Scott reached the Pole, he saw the Norwegian flag already flying; Amundsen had arrived thirty-one days earlier. Shocked and dejected, Scott headed back to his base. While Amundsen rode his sleds back to base camp, Scott and his four companions laboriously walked and occasionally skied toward their food cache at One Ton Depot. En route two died, and with only eleven miles to go, the last three, including Scott, froze to death.

By the time he planned his expedition to the South Pole, Byrd had already made headlines with three important feats.

First, he developed the sun compass and worked out the compilations for navigating a plane across the Atlantic to the Azores, a group of volcanic islands west of Portugal. For two months in 1926 he had lived in Trepassey Bay in Newfoundland, working with the three Navy-Curtiss planes that the U.S. Navy had assigned to fly the Atlantic. Byrd planned to navigate the lead plane. Hours before the flight, the Navy Department, concerned about the dangers of the undertaking, pulled Byrd and replaced his weight with additional fuel. But because he had already navigated the mission on paper, the Navy records gave Byrd full credit for the success of the flight.

Second, he flew from Kings Bay, Spitsbergen (a group of islands to the north of Norway), over the North Pole and back, a flight no one had ever tried before. He and another famous flyer, Floyd Bennett, were the first to reach the Pole by air.

Third, on June 29, 1927, Byrd flew the first multiengine plane across the Atlantic. It was also the first flight to carry overseas air mail.

Now, according to the *Transcript*, Byrd would take a party of forty men with him to Antarctica. The expedition would also conduct geographic and geological surveys. He expected to leave the United States by the fall of 1928, contingent on his raising half a million dollars to finance the trip. He was asking individuals and corporations to contribute.

"He plans to live there — in Antarctica — for a year!" I read a few paragraphs aloud. Had I stopped to think about my companions, I would have realized they were more interested in their homework than in Byrd's plans. But the news excited me, and I couldn't stop talking about the expedition.

"This will open up the South Pole," I said. "Think of the minerals that might be under the ice. The only land on earth not yet explored — and no American has ever set foot on Antarctica . . ."

"It'll be a history-making event, all right," Freddie Crockett said, dropping his head toward his books.

Eddie Goodale, my best friend since childhood and a fellow volunteer with Grenfell, expressed a mild interest. "Sounds like an exciting trip. Would be quite an adventure to go along. But how could you get on board?" He, too, returned to his books.

Silence descended on the room, broken only by the turning of a page or the scraping of a chair. I read the entire article and then reread it, pausing to daydream about being on that still-unexplored continent.

Having lived with Grenfell under Arctic conditions for eight months, I had some idea of life in a subzero land. Once again I could feel the sharp winds ripping mercilessly at my face, despite the fur hood of my parka. The sled dogs viciously scrapped among themselves yet were instantly ready to go out on the trail. Once again I tasted the food we had called hoosh, a concoction high in protein and fat, ideal because of the cold temperatures and the strenuous work of traversing rugged land. This fatty soup, with its generous portions of meat and spices, produced an aroma like nothing else in the world.

In imagination, I sniffed the air — clean and unsullied by factory smokestacks. The snow-covered ground remained white, disturbed only by the occasional prints of dogs, sleds, and skis.

"I've got to go!" I said. "I must go with Byrd!" In speaking those words aloud, I had made my decision. I would become part of Byrd's expedition even though I didn't have the slightest idea how to get invited. But I would find a way.

I was twenty-two years old, back at Harvard for the second time. On my return from Labrador, I had promised myself and my parents that I would study hard, make up my missed work, and graduate. Now, only a year after reenrollment, adventure beckoned again.

Priding myself on being in top condition, I was a husky six-footer who could meet any kind of physical demands. Having once proven it in the Arctic region, I was now ready for the ultimate test: living in Antarctica.

Young and infused with enthusiasm, I didn't allow a negative thought to influence me. Had I analyzed the situation, I would have realized that Byrd didn't have the funds to hire people. Not once did I ask myself why Byrd would want me with him. I didn't even stop to consider that taking off for another year would delay my career plans — and incur the disappointment and displeasure of my parents.

———————◆———————

"Sir, please help me. I *have* to go with Byrd to the South Pole."

"Yes, yes," McDonald said. "But I still don't quite understand why you came to me."

"Because you can get to Commander Byrd and tell him about me. If you talk to him, he'll listen and he'll take me."

Those words sound brash as I repeat them. Yet I honestly believed that once Byrd knew how badly I wanted to go on the expedition, he would naturally want me. I concluded, "I came here for one reason. I want your help. I'd like you to talk with Commander Byrd. Ask him to give me a chance. I will leave college immediately and travel to New Hampshire, where he is assembling his dogs and supplies."

When McDonald made no comment, I added my final salvo: "Tell Commander Byrd I'll leave for New Hampshire with absolutely no obligation on his part. Furthermore, I'm prepared to work for nothing for one year, driving dogs, training dog leaders, building their cages, and doing whatever is necessary to get those dogs ready for his expedition to the Antarctic. At the end of the year he can examine what I've done and then decide whether he wants to take me."

"I don't see how he could turn that offer down."

"That's why I made it, sir."

"I'm willing to do what I can," he said with kindness in his voice. "I'll contact Commander Byrd and tell him about you. Then I'll get back in touch and tell you what he says."

"Thank you, Mr. McDonald! Thank you!" I must have sounded foolish, thanking him again and again, but I meant it. McDonald was going to push the door open for me.

My worries of just the hour before disappeared. I knew Byrd wouldn't turn me down. He couldn't! Yet for the next two days I could hardly wait for McDonald's phone call. I cut all my classes and stayed in the dorm. Every time the phone rang, I rushed to answer it.

When McDonald finally phoned, he gave me a message that sounded more like a telegram: "Commander Byrd has accepted your proposition."

I was so overjoyed, I ran through the dorm, yelling at anyone who would listen. "I'm going! I'm going with Byrd to the South Pole!"

Once I calmed down, I knew that I had to tell my family before I could make any further plans. Although they hadn't fully approved, my parents had allowed me to drop out of Harvard to go with Grenfell.

9

Father, highly successful in business, understandably wanted me to get my degree, settle down, and lead a normal, productive life.

When I started out on the twenty-seven miles to our home in Hamilton, Massachusetts, that evening, I planned to arrive just as my parents finished dinner. Being a few minutes early, I waited outside, peeking through the dining room window, until I saw the butler take the coffee into the living room. That ritual was my cue. Mother and Father would come in immediately, and I could be alone with them.

Father, a large-framed man with a dark complexion, looked up in surprise as I entered. "Norman, what are you doing here? Aren't you supposed to be in college today?"

"Yes, but I had something important to discuss with you." I sat down across from him. Mother poured a cup of coffee and handed it to me.

Father listened while I told him about Byrd's expedition to the South Pole. I rushed on, not giving him a chance to interrupt or argue me out of it. Mother, who said nothing then or later, listened with a helpless expression of dismay. Despite my enthusiastic commitment, I hated myself for bringing sadness and disappointment to her life. While she had given me nothing but encouragement and affection, I was causing her misery by departing from what she wanted me to do. Believing a college education was the best thing for me, Mother wanted me to finish my schooling before I did anything else. She had silently given in when I went to Labrador, and now I was asking her approval for a second postponement, one that was potentially life-threatening.

Speaking with more bravado than I felt, I said, "Father, I want to go on this expedition. I must go. It's the most important thing in the world to me. I know it's a disappointment to both of you, but it's something I must do."

"You feel that strongly about going, do you?" he asked.

"Oh, yes," I said. "As a matter of fact, I've already told Commander Byrd I would go." Naturally, I didn't tell him the conditions under which Byrd had accepted me. As I explained my role in the expedition, not once did he offer an opinion or state how he felt.

When I stopped, he looked up at me and asked several practical questions. "Norman, have you met Byrd himself?"

"No, not yet. He sent me a message, though."

"When will you meet him?"

"He'll be coming to New Hampshire to meet me."

Finally came the question I had dreaded: "What kind of salary are you going to receive?"

"No salary," I said.

Even if I hadn't known Father well, his startled expression would have told me that my answer was not what he wanted to hear.

"Do I perceive this correctly?" he asked quietly. "You will have no salary from Commander Byrd, even though you'll work for him for a year before you leave for Antarctica? Who'll take care of your expenses?"

His question hinted that I had won his approval, even if reluctantly given. More confident now, I said, "Don't worry, Father. Commander Byrd is going to take care of me."

"I see." Father turned to Mother and said, "We won't need to send him his allowance then, will we?"

I hadn't counted on that response. My parents sent me $25 a week—a good sum in those days. I just assumed that once they had granted me permission, they would continue to send my living allowance. But I couldn't backtrack. Besides, I had overcome my two big obstacles: Byrd had accepted me, and my parents had acquiesced. Nothing would stop me now.

As I drove away, stark reality set in. I faced one hell of a problem. I would be gone a year, and I would have to eat. What would I do without money? I would have to solve that problem once I reached New Hampshire.

Three Musketeers

"**I**'m going to work for Commander Byrd! I'm going to the South Pole!" The words rang through my head, and I had visions of adventure and hardship in that cold land. Most of all, I kept thinking of the privilege of being included in the expedition. And Byrd would invite me after he saw my work. Not once during the months ahead would I have doubts about his taking me.

After speaking with my parents, I returned to Harvard for the night. The next morning, without bothering to withdraw from my classes, I collected all my things from the dorm and drove home a second time. Mother sadly helped me pack my clothes. With my five dogs as companions, I drove my Ford from Hamilton to Wonalancet, New Hampshire. No one knew I was coming, and it hadn't occurred to me to inform anyone.

I decided I'd go directly to Arthur Walden, whom I had known for some time. According to McDonald's newspaper article, he was in charge of what Byrd called "assembling the dogs," or acquiring and training the dogs for the expedition.

When I arrived in Wonalancet late that afternoon, I had no food, a few dollars in my pocket, and no more money to come. Byrd hadn't said anything about when I should arrive or where I'd be housed. Anyway, I was too excited about being there to let practical matters trouble me. I drove immediately to the inn owned by Walden and his wife, Kate. Their inn, like dozens of other such places, catered to the wealthy who spent portions of their winter enjoying the skiing.

Walden's face registered surprise at seeing me, but I didn't give him a chance to question my being there or to refuse to let me stay. "Commander Byrd agreed that I should come here and help you work with the dogs," I said.

Walden was a short man in his late fifties, but he moved with the vigor of a younger man. Although I did not know him well, I recognized that he had a tremendous ability with animals: The dogs responded to him extraordinarily well. He had raised a good leader named Chinook, the chance offspring of a German shepherd and an Eskimo dog, and from Chinook he had started breeding a successful line of sled dogs. The Chinooks, as he called the breed, were strong, yet gentle with people.

For several minutes we talked about trivial things because Walden, I sensed, was trying to figure out what to do with me. Obviously, he wasn't prepared for me, and just as obviously he wasn't going to offer me a room in his inn. Aside from his initial shock, I couldn't tell from his face or voice how he felt, but he didn't display any antagonism, and I assumed that at worst he looked on me as a nuisance he would have to put up with.

"Well, we've got to do something about you, Norman," he said. He opened the door, and I followed him outside. We walked across the grounds behind the inn. The maples and oaks, nearly barren, hinted of cold weather to come. I enjoyed hearing the gold and red leaves crunching under our feet.

He pointed to the gazebo. "That's all I can offer you — it's the only place that's not in use."

"That's fine." Sleeping practically outdoors in a gazebo would be my first challenge on the job. Instead of being unhappy, I was secretly glad. I constantly sought ways to toughen myself, and this was a perfect way to begin.

The inn's gazebo, used for afternoon teas in summer, was a flat porch elevated on piers four feet above the ground and surrounded with glass and screening. It stood on the bank of a stream and overlooked the dog yard. While providing only slight protection from the chilling winter temperatures and winds, the gazebo did have a roof and an open fireplace for guests to enjoy informal fall gatherings.

Walden started to apologize for not having anything better. "I didn't know you were coming—"

I stopped him by saying, "I'll manage with no problem."

Before he left me, I said, "Arthur, how about a job working in the dining room? You know, work for my food?" I didn't tell him that I had no money.

"Kate and I don't have anything to do with that part," he said. "You'll have to talk to the cook."

As I soon learned, although the kitchen and dining room operated under Kate's name, the cook ran them both. She managed the place as if she owned it and was strict about everything.

Determined not to tell the cook or anyone that I had made no provision to eat, I asked for a job as a dishwasher. I figured I could do that as payment for my food.

"We have a dishwasher." She turned away from me.

"How about a busboy?"

"Don't need one."

I finally persuaded her to take me on as a waiter, even though I had no experience. My duties included setting the large table, keeping the area clean, and sweeping up afterward. The pay was absolutely zero, but I figured I'd be able to survive on the leftovers.

Having talked my way into the job, I was very pleased with myself. Then the cook said, "You don't touch any of the leftovers that come back to the kitchen on the serving platters. We need every scrap of food they don't eat. I use it all the next day in some form. And that includes desserts. You understand?"

"Yes—"

"And if I catch you eating anything off the platters, I'll fire you."

I would have to revise my thinking. By dinnertime, however, I had come up with a plan and was eager to try it out. I was also hungry.

We had lamb, and my responsibility was to cut the meat and then serve it. I cut the meat carefully, and carrying it on a large platter with potatoes and English peas, I went into the dining area. The cook had instructed me to serve the guests one at a time, ladies first.

Approaching the first woman, I asked, "Ma'am, would you care for lamb?"

"Oh, yes," she said, "I love lamb."

She received a small piece on her plate and equally small portions of mashed potatoes and peas. I went completely around the large table that way, giving each of them meager servings. As I expected, they cleaned their plates.

I went around a second time. "More lamb, ma'am?"

"Yes," the woman said. "That first piece was delicious."

This time she received the biggest piece of lamb from the platter. I offered everyone massive second helpings. While they were eating, I took the unserved food back to the kitchen. There was very little on the platters.

When I returned to the dining room, I found just what I wanted: The guests had left large portions of food on their plates. I scraped the uneaten lamb onto one plate, potatoes onto a second, and vegetables onto a third. I had an excellent meal.

———————◆———————

After a week of working, I telephoned my college roommate, Eddie Goodale (collect, of course). "Eddie, you need to be here and become part of this." Enthusiastically, I told him about the preparations for the expedition. "You'll love it. We drive the dogs every day. You can live outdoors with me in a gazebo with an open fireplace."

Eddie got caught up in my excitement, and he asked the practical kind of questions. How could he get on the team? How could he see Commander Byrd?

"I don't know how you go about all of those things," I said. "Why don't you take a gamble? Just show up."

As crazy as it may sound, that's exactly what Eddie did. When I vouched for him, Walden let him stay on. About that time the dishwasher got sick and went home for good. Eddie joined with me, and together we did everything except cook the food. Since Eddie didn't have any money, either, we used the same solution to get his food. By then, a few of the guests had figured out what we were doing and were leaving generous portions on their plates. After that, very little food went back on the platters.

A week after Eddie's arrival, we enlisted another classmate, Freddie Crockett. Walden didn't turn him away, either, once Freddie agreed to sleep with us in the gazebo. People soon dubbed us the three musketeers. Later, even Byrd would call us that.

Making a real adventure out of living in the gazebo, we jokingly reminded ourselves, "This is good training. We'll be able to endure the cold and the tough life better than anyone else."

During the winter we used the open fireplace only when the temperature turned bitterly cold. We had to cut the wood, and we didn't get much heat out of so inefficient a source. Harsh winds whistled right through every crack. Not very comfortable living, but I loved it. Eddie enjoyed living in the gazebo as much as I did, and Freddie fitted right in with us. We sat up in the well-warmed workshop at night when we wanted to read. But when it was time to go to bed, we hurried over to the gazebo and leapt inside our sleeping bags.

Back at college, my friend Sam Burns was monitor (attendance checker) in History I. Not wanting to give me a "cut-class" report, he marked me present. This favor continued for most of the semester. One night Sam went to the movies. The *Pathe News* — a regular feature in those days — showed a segment on "the Three Musketeers from Harvard driving their dogs in preparation for the South Pole."

The next day Vaughan was marked absent.

First thing every morning, we cleaned up the dog yard. Then, going into the warm workshop and away from the cook's eyes, we ate our confiscated food from the night before. We had to make each portion last: The inn served only one hot meal a day.

As our top priority, we trained our dogs. We also prepared special leather and webbing harnesses and equipped our sleds with sled sheets, which would keep cargo from spilling out as we sped around turns but could also function like sails on a ship, allowing winds to propel the sled and help the dogs. Walden shared the expertise he had picked up in the Yukon, where he had freighted supplies for the gold miners. From him we learned to tie and lash down different kinds of cargo—lumber, boxes, kegs of nails, long timbers, dog food, bags of coal—and to tie various kinds of knots. He showed us how to pack supplies for the two expedition ships as well.

We learned to sew leather overmitts with huge gauntlets to slip over the cuffs of our parkas. An attempt to use fox pelts around the edges of our parka hoods proved unworkable because the fur matted easily from the moisture in our exhaled breath. Just before we left New Hampshire, Byrd got us high-quality clothing from Nome, Alaska: pants made from the legs of caribou, caribou parkas, sleeping bags, mittens, and mukluks (Eskimo moccasins). We wore everything à la Eskimo except the rabbit skin underwear. While warm enough, rabbit skin was too hairy, constantly matted, and wasn't washable on the trail.

Later, the caribou hair would pose a continuous problem on the ice. The hair was everywhere—in our woolen underwear, in our shirts, in our eyes, and even in our soup. But it provided the warmth we needed, so we didn't complain too often.

We worked hard from September 1927 until the fall of 1928 getting ready for the expedition. One time the three of us drove to Canada and picked up dogs that a ship had brought down for the Byrd expedition. We met the boat, immediately inspected and inoculated the animals, and drove them back to New Hampshire. By the time we left for the South Pole, we had ninety-seven dogs trained and ready.

———————◆———————

I'll never forget my first encounter with Byrd. Although he had agreed to my terms to work for nothing, we still had not met. He visited

18

the camp at Wonalancet specifically to meet me and my two friends.

Byrd wore his Navy uniform and appeared friendly. I immediately liked his looks. A thin, medium-sized man, he exuded power. Even when speaking quietly, his low voice demanded attention, and his appearance suggested a man in his early thirties, ten years younger than his real age.

After Walden introduced us, Byrd said, "I'd like to see the dogs."

We three musketeers had worked hard to train them, and we knew we had done a good job. Byrd approached the dogs and Walden followed behind him as if they were going through a military inspection. He walked around, observing the animals from several angles, saying nothing, puffing on his pipe. He bent down and scrutinized one or two dogs, then moved on. Using only his eyes, he examined every dog we had trained. During the entire procedure, Byrd never said a word.

When he finished, he smiled, and I saw the excitement in his face. "You've done an excellent job. I'm pleased."

Later that day he again told us that he liked the way we had taken care of the dogs. Then we heard the words we had waited for: "And I would like you three musketeers to accompany us to Antarctica."

"Thank you, sir," each of us managed to say, too overcome to add anything more.

As soon as he was out of sight, Eddie and Freddie went into frenzied laughing and shouting, but my excitement didn't quite match theirs. I felt a little disappointed that I didn't feel more buoyed. I've since figured that I *knew* I was going to the Pole with Byrd all along. I had decided so the day I read the newspaper headline.

Byrd recognized our innovations and expressed his gratitude. We had done everything we could think of to make the expedition more successful. In particular, Byrd thanked us for two things we did on our own.

First, we made by hand an igloo-shaped tent. So far as we knew, no previous explorer had ever used a tent that shape. (Now, every camping supplier offers dome tents.) We tested its effectiveness by erecting the tent in the middle of a field, where we would get the full force of the wind, and sleeping in it. As we figured, the whistling winds circled around instead of pummeling the flat surfaces. When the wind strikes a regular tent, a battle ensues to see who wins. In high winds, the forces of nature succeed, and the structure crumples. But our dome tent had no large flat surfaces. To make it even better, we sewed in the two stakes so that we could fold the whole thing as one piece and pack it easily and quickly on our sleds.

Second, we worked out a formula for dog food and the amount necessary for ninety-seven dogs. We calculated how much food each dog would need while living on the ice, as well as for the trip down and back by ship. We would not need a full supply at our base camp in Antarctica because we would have the best dog food in the world available to us: seal meat, which has fat for warmth and protein for strength.

We worked with a chemist, Milton Seeley, to figure out the formula these dogs would require. After several months of trying out different combinations, we favored one, and the dogs liked it. Our goal was to have the food made into biscuits, which meant we wouldn't have to cook their food.

A dog food company took the formula and agreed to donate forty thousand pounds—enough for the trip. Initially, the company sent us two tons to make sure it was what we wanted. This supply provided enough food for our dogs until we left the United States.

When we assured the makers that the dog biscuits were fine, they in turn contracted with the providers of the raw materials, who also agreed to donate their goods. The biscuits were packed in waterproof containers for the diverse climates the ship would go through and sent directly to Norfolk, Virginia, for loading onto a mother ship of the Norwegian whaling fleet going to Antarctica via New Zealand.

We felt proud of ourselves for working out this formula, which made excellent food for the dogs. Unfortunately, we really hadn't taken care of the dogs' food. As we would learn, and I especially, a lot of troubles were in store for us.

The Black Gang

My most emotional moment in the year of preparation came the night before we left Wonalancet. Father drove up alone to say good-bye. We talked a few minutes and then, just before he left, he embraced me. For him it was a tremendous expression of affection; Father did not easily express his love. It was all the more amazing because he had not shown any enthusiasm about my going on the expedition. The unexpected embrace made me realize how deeply he cared about me.

As Father hugged me, I felt him place something in my hand. I glanced down and saw his gold Hamilton watch. He had carried that timepiece for sixteen years. On the inside cover was an etching of my sister, his only daughter.

"Father, you shouldn't give me this—"

"Take it," he said. "I want you to have it."

He didn't have tears in his eyes—my father was too self-controlled for that—but the huskiness of his voice let me know how hard he was working to exert that control.

"Thank you, Father," I said lamely. "I'll take good care of it." I knew how much he treasured the watch. It represented a level of affection for me that he could never put into words. I wore the watch outside my underwear throughout my trip to Antarctica. It hung by a buckskin lanyard.

Through many lonely times on the ice, especially during the long nights, I thought of that priceless gift from my father. It always made me feel a little closer to him and to Mother.

———◆———

The next day we three musketeers left by train for Norfolk, Virginia. We traveled in a freight car with ninety-seven dogs in individual crates, twenty heavy freight sleds, dog harnesses, various kinds of winter gear, and three drums of water for the dogs, each holding fifty-five gallons.

Byrd had highly advertised this historic expedition, regularly sending out news items about its progress. He made sure the people of New Hampshire knew our train route: The newspapers printed the schedule of our ride through the state. To our delighted surprise, at every station in New Hampshire the train stopped with our freight car right at the loading platform. Well-wishers, anywhere from fifty to one hundred fifty people, waited for us, calling to us by name and waving, wishing us success on the trip. Several of them thrust home-cooked food into our hands. They shouted their encouragement; a few said they wished they were going along. At one station, a troop of Boy Scouts came to salute and send their good wishes to Paul Siple, the Eagle Scout who had won a Scouting competition to go with Byrd.

We were supposed to stay on the train for three days; the trip took considerably longer. Somehow the railroad people made a mistake and misattached our freight car to a westward-bound train. When we awakened after our first night, expecting to be halfway to Norfolk, we learned we had reached Detroit instead.

The railroad company realized the mistake and apologized several times, but the error didn't dampen our spirits because the delay wouldn't affect our leaving the country. Even with the lost time, we would still have a few days in Norfolk. Since none of us had ever been west, we readily accepted the extra ride as one more part of our adventure. Other than enduring the monotony of such a confined space, we were comfortable: At night we used sleeping bags placed on the floor, and during the day we lounged on top of the dog crates. The good people in New Hampshire had kindly provided plenty of delicious food. Our only responsibilities entailed feeding and watering the dogs. Occasionally, I picked up a book, but I couldn't concentrate and finally gave up trying. Through the cracked-open freight door, scenery such as we had never seen before whizzed by, mesmerizing us for most of the daylight hours.

On our arrival at Norfolk, workers unloaded the equipment and our dogs into a dockside shed. Knowing it would be several more days before the ship finished loading up a year's supplies for the South Pole, we alternated staying with the dogs, one of us remaining while the others visited with friends and family members who had traveled by passenger train to Norfolk. My mother came to see me, and her presence made it a special send-off. We three musketeers relished our four days of dining in luxurious restaurants, a drastic contrast to Wonalancet. Even nicer, we slept in a hotel — the last sleep in a comfortable bed any of us would have for a long, long time.

Four days later the dog drivers and teams boarded the Norwegian whaler *Sir James Clark Ross,* a mother ship with eight chasers. These faster vessels ran down whales, harpooned and killed them, then pumped their carcasses full of air so they would stay afloat. The slower mother ship retrieved the whales while the chasers steamed after more prey.

We hitched a ride on the whaler's annual trip from Norway to the Antarctic, which made a special port of call to pick us up at Norfolk and transport us to Port Chalmers, New Zealand's southernmost port. Byrd put us on the *Ross* because that ship would get the dogs through the tropics faster. The huskies would suffer badly from the equatorial heat. Byrd also chose the coal-burning ship because of its big, flat deck: two hundred and ten feet. We could take our dogs out of the crates to exercise them daily.

Byrd himself and the rest of the crew sailed on the *City of New York,* a wooden ship so named as a compliment to the city fathers, who had given storage and berthing space to the expedition in New York Harbor. A small steamer, named the *Eleanor Bolling* after Byrd's mother, followed. The trip itself posed no problems. The dog food, however, brought calamity and panic to our party. We had no inkling of the disaster until the first night out of Norfolk, when we fed our dogs the food we had ordered from Wonalancet.

None of us paid any special attention when we put the food out for the dogs. But instead of tearing into it with their usual healthy appetites, the dogs refused to eat. They sniffed their rations a few times and turned their heads away.

Despite our urgings to eat, they backed away, refusing to get close to the biscuits. The few who ate more than a few bites developed diarrhea during the night.

Obviously, something was wrong. At first we thought it might be the dogs themselves. But why would all ninety-seven hate the food?

Inspecting the biscuits, I immediately realized that it didn't even look like what we had been feeding them at Wonalancet. Yet the dog food company was supposed to have followed the same formula.

"Look at this!" I yelled angrily. I cracked open two biscuits and showed them to Goodale and Crockett. Disgusted, I threw them against the bulkhead of the ship. I checked another handful. It was the same. The biscuits contained all kinds of foreign matter from glass to wire, dirt, string, pieces of cloth, and paper. It looked to me as if the suppliers had thrown in the floor sweepings from their factories.

"What is going on here?" I asked. "We can't use one damn biscuit of this mess!" We opened a dozen bags at random. "Forty thousand pounds and it's totally useless!"

After our return to America we learned what had happened. The company that donated the dog food had appealed to the suppliers of the various ingredients for donations. The suppliers had agreed, but they sent inferior products. Unaware of the impurity of the donated products, the manufacturer had mixed, baked, packaged, and transported the forty thousand pounds to Norfolk.

The manufacturer remained ignorant of the fact that our whole expedition nearly collapsed because of the inedible dog food. Had our animals been on the slower boats with the rest of the men, enduring the heat of the tropics, the diarrhea, and the long voyage, many of them would have died. And had we not discovered the situation until we reached Antarctica, the loss of the dogs would have ended the expedition before it even began.

Fortunately, when leaving New Hampshire, we had taken along the leftover dog food, a fairly good amount, and put it aboard the whaler. It provided a minimal diet for the dogs throughout the trip. We supplemented the biscuits by begging food from the crew's galley, gratefully accepting anything they would give us. In addition, we cooked oatmeal, cornmeal, and potatoes. The dogs especially appreciated the fish we fed them four times a week. Still, because of inadequate diet, the animals lost weight, and their coats lost their healthy sheen.

Upon landing, we immediately put our dogs on Quarantine Island, where they were to stay until we left for the ice. We purchased dog food locally and sent it to the island. It was a light summer mixture with little fat, quite inadequate to take with us because of the heavy demands the Antarctic would place on the animals. To supplement the commercial food, we boiled rice and cornmeal and mixed it with tallow. Although it was too caloric for a long stretch in warm weather, they loved it and began to put the weight back on.

Best of all, no dogs died from this experience.

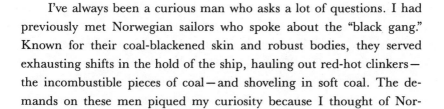

I've always been a curious man who asks a lot of questions. I had previously met Norwegian sailors who spoke about the "black gang." Known for their coal-blackened skin and robust bodies, they served exhausting shifts in the hold of the ship, hauling out red-hot clinkers — the incombustible pieces of coal — and shoveling in soft coal. The demands on these men piqued my curiosity because I thought of Norwegian seamen as tough.

When we went aboard the *Sir James Clark Ross,* the captain invited us to eat with him at his table. We sat down in our working clothes and chatted as we ate.

I mentioned the black gang and said, "I've heard that their work is tough. Is their job really the hardest job on the ship?"

"On the ship?" he said in his accented English. "More than that. It is the hardest physical job in the world. They must work under the worst conditions possible."

Without stopping to reason it out, and being impetuous by nature, I said, "Captain, could I join your black gang?"

He scowled in shock. "You are joking? You want to shovel coal?"

"I've never done it before. But I'd like to try it."

He smiled. I'm sure he thought that a few hours down there would change my mind.

"I'm serious. I want to work hard on this trip. I want to be in top physical condition when we get to the Antarctic."

"It is the most backbreaking job. The sweat, the grime, the —"

"I still want to do it."

"You cannot mean this." He reflected a few seconds, the scowl imprinted on his face. "This is not the work for a person like you."

"I'm totally serious." As I spoke, I realized that the others at the table had stopped talking and everyone was listening.

Goodale nudged me. "Are you crazy?"

I turned to him. "Maybe. But I still want to do it." I looked directly into the captain's deep-blue eyes. "I want to join the black gang."

"I will have to speak with the engineer. He must agree to take you down there. You understand, the work is hard and also very dangerous."

"I still want to do it," I persisted. I asked Goodale and Crockett to care for my dogs until we reached New Zealand. They agreed.

The next morning I talked with the engineer, who spoke a limited amount of English. He made it clear that he also thought I was insane.

Finally, he said, "You follow me." He led me into the bowels of the whaling ship. We went down an endless number of open-tread iron steps. The closer we got to the boiler room, the higher the temperature.

He stopped and pointed to the men working at the boilers. "Now do you want to come down and live here with them?"

I watched the men, fascinated by the speed at which they worked in that intense heat. A tall, muscular man walked through the boiler room, completely naked and wet with sweat. He didn't have an ounce of fat on his body. He looked like the toughest, most physically fit man I had ever seen.

"Is he one of the black gang?"

"Yes."

I knew then that I wanted to stay. He was a perfect example of how that kind of demanding labor builds bodies. "I'm ready to go to work. Today."

He shook his head for a long time, as if not believing what he had heard. "You can try if you must," he said at last.

Like the captain, he figured that after a few hours I'd get tired and want to go back up with the rest of the expedition crew.

Before the engineer left me, he explained to the black gang that I would join them. I went topside, moved out of my assigned quarters, and hurried below decks to the fo'c'sle to stay with the gang.

For the first few days, the black gang members regarded me with skepticism. Once they realized I was going to stick with the task, I became part of the crew. And I felt proud to be accepted.

I learned quickly that I *had* taken on the hardest physical job in the world. Certainly it was the most demanding work I had ever done — or would ever do again.

We shoveled coal into the boilers and raked out the clinkers at full speed. The whaling ship had three boilers, two operating while one cooled off to be cleaned.

After all these years I can still smell the dust and feel the grime from that boiler room as the soot settled on my skin. I can hear the hissing of the clinkers as they splashed onto the wet steel deck.

They lent me the black-gang uniform. Because of the torturous heat, we wore only three articles of clothing: a wide jockstrap, a large neckerchief, and wooden-soled sandals.

The neckerchiefs were to wipe from our faces the continuous perspiration running down our foreheads and into our eyes and mouth. No matter how tightly we twisted the cloth afterward, we could never wring out all the moisture. As soon as we started to work again, the cloth was wet. The jockstrap took the place of heavy clothes we would otherwise have had around our legs. The wooden-soled sandals lifted us a full inch above the steel deck. Only a toe strap over the instep kept them on our feet as we moved around.

I soon understood that, paradoxical as it may sound, we wore sandals so that our feet would not get burned. When we hauled hot clinkers out of the boiler, they hit the deck, and sparks spattered. If a spark landed on a closed shoe, it would stay there and burn right through to the skin. Because of the ever-present intense heat, we wouldn't have felt it before we suffered a serious burn. With sandals, the instant a clinker hit a bare foot, we could move quickly away. Nevertheless, like all apprentices, I sustained a few burns when I first started. Those incidents taught me to move back a little faster when I raked out.

The clinkers fell eighteen inches from the bottom sill of the boiler door onto the steel deck. We waited until they were cold enough to handle before we shoveled them into iron buckets. When full, the buckets went up the wind chute to the upper deck and were dumped over the leeward side of the ship.

It was always a relief when the last clinker came out and we scooped up all the ashes into the bucket. Then we turned to the black, dusty, soft coal and shoveled it into the boiler, carefully spreading it around.

At the end of every operation, either filling a boiler with coal or cleaning one out, I had a chance to rinse my body. It felt so good . . . momentarily. Sometimes I soaked my face in cold salt water. Like the others, I took long drinks of the plentiful drinking water, and it amazed me how wonderful it tasted after all that evaporation of moisture from my body.

The meals and sleeping arrangements were confusing to me at first because I did not speak any Norwegian except "ya" and "nay." I didn't have an opportunity to pick up the language, so for the entire forty days, I interpreted the black gang more by their gestures than by their words.

Without exception they treated me with kindness. I'm sure they wondered why this crazy American was working alongside them. I was younger than any of them, and they probably wanted to make sure I was all right. It may have been partly pride, but I was determined to carry my own load. After the first day, no one had to help me keep up.

But for the first week, at the end of my shift, I was too exhausted to do anything except eat and sleep. Working not only hard and continually but also in the intense heat with poor ventilation sapped my strength.

Since the boilers had to run twenty-four hours a day, we had alternating shifts. The watches were four hours on and four hours off. When my turn came to sleep, I would stagger back to the bunks, wondering whether I would ever have the strength to walk or bend again. A black gang member would roll out of his bunk and I would crawl in. I always had the same bunk — but only for four hours. I can laugh now about the sleeping situation. It was part of the adventure, and I was so dead tired, I didn't care what the accommodations were.

All the black gang ate at the same table. I lost a lot of weight, all fat. Once I became acclimated, I felt as strong as any of the lifetime black gang members.

We had good food in abundant amounts. I especially remember the goat cheese and crackers and the inexhaustible supply of coffee. The others watched out for me, making certain I had a full plate with plenty of bread and butter in front of me.

We had radioed Commander Byrd about the useless dog food, and he had sent back a simple but direct order: "Fix it."

I offered to go to the city of Dunedin — near Port Chalmers, our port of call in New Zealand — to see what I could do with manufacturers and friends of Byrd's. Properly it should have been Walden's job, since he was in charge of the dogs. But he wasn't up to handling that kind of emergency. He was a former dog driver from Alaska, nearing retirement when Byrd asked him to collect and head up the dogs for the expedition. He was a good man at what he did, but he did not know how to make decisions quickly or how to delegate responsibility.

Arthur Walden and I had a speaking but wary relationship. Almost from the beginning, it was obvious that Walden didn't particularly like the three musketeers. Compared with him, we were educated and came from wealthy families. This disparity made him feel inferior. I won't say that we didn't feel a little smug at times because we probably did. He accused us of having "smart ideas" while he concentrated on the fundamentals of life. He was good at taking care of the dogs, however, and at doing his job. But he lacked the ability to look ahead and to foresee difficulties, and to me that meant he lacked leadership ability.

Because Walden had no idea what to do about the dogs' food supply, I think he felt relieved when I took over. But his relief had a sharp edge to it. He became jealous and angry. I had no inkling of what my volunteering to take care of the food would do to Walden.

After we reached New Zealand and I went to Dunedin, Byrd talked with me through his business agent about the dogs' food. Byrd was enough of a leader to recognize Walden's value but also his limitations. It pleased me immensely that the commander appreciated my jumping in to solve the problem.

I proposed a simple plan. By collecting the necessary ingredients, we could use the formula we had developed in Wonalancet and make the food ourselves. We would pack it into two-pound squares—roughly the daily needs of one dog. When Byrd heard my idea, he gave me the go-ahead.

Naturally, the more attention I received, the more Walden felt overlooked. Perhaps he thought I purposely did things to ingratiate myself with Byrd. So far as I know, I didn't have that kind of motive, although I am human and competitive enough to try to do a job better than anyone else.

Even when I finally understood what was happening to Walden, I don't think I cared much. Being ambitious and hard working, I had an attitude of move-out-of-the-way-if-you-can't-do-the-job. From what he said to others later, it became apparent that Walden believed I schemed to push him aside.

———————◆———————

Expeditions cost money. Byrd financed the trip through donations from individuals and corporations. He had no funds to buy food for the animals. At the time we landed in Dunedin he was fifty thousand dollars in debt. The lack of money didn't trouble me. I knew from our experience in America that people would respond if they knew the need.

I went to the newspapers in Port Chalmers and Dunedin (about fifteen miles away) and told them our story. They wrote an account of our dilemma and showered us with publicity. Because of the free advertising, we raised every cent we needed for the ingredients before we left for Antarctica. The suppliers kindly sold their products to us at cost and donated more on top of that. We figured we got all our ingredients at about twenty percent of their actual cost.

My most serious problem centered on how to do the mixing. I needed a place big enough to store the ingredients. My plan was to prepare the dog food in troughs with a shovel, the way we mixed cement.

Hudson Brothers Chocolate Factory came to our rescue. Because they did their mixing and baking during the day, they could give us the use of their machines at night as long as I was out of the way and had the mixers cleaned by seven o'clock in the morning.

I faithfully provided spotless equipment when the factory workers arrived each morning. I didn't have much choice: Under the meticulous scrutiny of the supervisor, I worked at steaming and scrubbing the mixers until they passed inspection.

For eleven hours a night, twenty-five straight nights, I mixed fish meal, meat meal, beef tallow, wheat germ, molasses, and cod liver oil. Next, I molded this mixture into meat cakes that looked like bricks.

A personal problem confronted me: I had received no money from Byrd or any other source. That left me with no place to live in Dunedin and no money for my own food. It was too far to go back and forth to Port Chalmers every night. Having no other place, I slept in the factory at different spots where it was quiet and I could stretch out. I didn't ask for permission, but no one challenged my sleeping arrangements. I had a sleeping bag, and that's all I needed.

There was still the problem of food. At first I ate the leftover products from the chocolate factory: chocolate-covered biscuits, chocolate wafers, and best of all, chocolate-dipped doughnuts. The workers, realizing my situation, started bringing me food from their homes, and soon I was eating better than my friends on Quarantine Island.

31

———————◆———————

By the time we left Port Chalmers, I was eager to see Antarctica. It would be a dream fulfilled and an opportunity few other people would ever have.

Only one thing marred the trip: Arthur Walden. I became increasingly aware of his sullenness toward me. The episode with the dogs' food had widened an already apparent breach between us.

Had I been more sensitive, I might have tried to get along better with him. But I didn't think about him often. And when I did, I figured he was the one who had a problem.

That was only the beginning. It would not be many days before the man made me actually fear for my life.

Little America

My concern for the dogs kept me watching over them as if they were my own children. We brought the animals on a barge from Quarantine Island to Dunedin. I helped the crew load them onto the wooden-decked *City of New York*. With a dog in every crate, we stacked the wooden boxes all over the upper decks, leaving only a passageway.

In the two days of loading dogs and equipment I worried about every one of the ninety-seven dogs. Had a bad storm arisen during the first few days out, many of them would have been washed overboard. Fortunately, the weather held until we had nailed down all the crates. We also added lines and straps to hold them secure. Yet the dogs' safety eased only part of my concern.

At sea the dogs suffered and moaned when the giant waves splashed across the deck and through some of their crates. Sled dogs have a thick undercoat that withstands cold temperatures, but their coats lack the oiliness of such dogs as the Chesapeake Bay and Labrador retrievers, which can stand in salt water up to their heads. These poor sled dogs suffered immensely from the chilling sting of the water.

I could do nothing about the situation except to watch carefully and check on them. Once we passed through the rough waters of the South Pacific and moved into the pack-ice belt, we hit calmer seas. The dogs dried out, ate better, and started to feel friskier. By the time we reached the Bay of Whales, they were in good condition. And the Dunedin-made food had passed the obvious test.

When we entered the pack ice, I had another opportunity to test my physical prowess. On December 16, Sverre Strom, first mate and copilot of the *City,* announced he was going into the crow's-nest.

The crow's-nest, made from a hogshead barrel, was close to the top of the mainmast. Heavy iron strapping around the mast kept it in place. When the ships entered the pack ice, someone had to go aloft to spot icebergs and signal the helmsman below.

"I want to go with you," I said.

"You must be out of your mind!" Strom's response sounded like that of the Norwegian whaler captain only weeks before. When I persisted, he admonished me. "You know nothing about ice piloting, Norm. It's boring. It's dangerous, too."

"I'm not afraid," I said. I don't know if I was or not. It was something I wanted to do; going aloft presented another challenge.

"I can't be responsible if anything happens —"

"I don't want you to be responsible. I want you to let me go with you."

"You'd have to stay up there a long time. Thirty-six hours with no sleep. Once you go up, you stay until I come down. Agreed?"

"Agreed!" I was elated at having an opportunity for another new experience.

Standing watch along with everyone else, I had climbed to the lower yardarms on several occasions. Getting to the crow's-nest at the top of the mainmast required careful footwork. Not being as agile as Sverre and never having climbed as high before, I was slow. The ship was rolling, and when I glanced down, we were over water on the starboard side. I looked a moment later, and we hung over water on the port side. I felt plenty scared, but I wouldn't have admitted it. To cover up, I laughed and yelled to Goodale and Crockett below.

Suddenly the roll stopped because we had entered the pack ice. This pack ice had been the barrier to Antarctic exploration. Once into the belt of ice, ships ran great risks of being crushed. Hence, until this century, little was known of the great land mass surrounding the South Pole.

Winter-frozen sea water in bays, harbors, estuaries, and in the shelter of islands breaks up in the summer. This broken ice then floats northward, away from the landfast ice. The ice moving from the Weddell Sea and the Ross Sea meets the currents of the Pacific, Atlantic, and Indian oceans and converges into a belt that encircles the continent. This pack ice extends ten to one hundred and fifty miles, depending on storms, currents, and the volume of ice broken off along the coastline. When the currents are strong enough to pack the ice together, ships don't even attempt to get through. A ship that gets caught may be caught for good. Steel ships are especially vulnerable because under pressure, their rivets pop and their welds crack; wooden ships can withstand pressure better. Ultimately, however, the ice will crush and sink any vessel.

Another hazard comes in the form of icebergs, which are formed by the calving of glaciers at the edge of the Ross Ice Barrier. These icebergs are often driven by strong underwater currents. If a ship is caught fast in the pack ice and an iceberg bears down upon it, there is no escape.

Now we had a job — an important one — to look for icebergs. Dark spots on the horizon mirrored open water, which is what we moved toward.

In the ensuing hours I occasionally wished Sverre hadn't let me go up with him. We remained in the crow's-nest for the full thirty-six hours. It was December, when we had no night — just daylight and sunshine all the time. I struggled with boredom, fatigue, and lack of mobility. From the galley they sent up our food in a swaying bucket. It was hot and we ate hungrily.

We did the only two things available to us up there. We searched the horizon with our eyes, and we talked. Sverre told me stories of hunting polar bears in Spitsbergen. I heard his sad tales of a sailor's hard life along with several of the dangerous episodes in his long career. His adventures fascinated me. Later, on the ice, I learned he was as brave as his tales suggested. In the ensuing months he earned the respect and admiration of all the others in our expedition.

His talking kept us both awake. Occasionally Sverre closed his eyes. Almost instantly he opened them again and seemed to be refreshed from the exercise. I didn't trust myself to try that.

We had to stand because we had no place to sit. Standing helped us to stay awake. Sometimes I'd sway back and forth or try any kind of physical motion to force myself to stay alert. Our job was critical to the safety of the ship. Sverre directed the ship through commands to the helmsman. "Six degrees to port!" he would call. Or, "Ten degrees starboard!"

The icebergs we encountered were long and flat-topped, peculiar to the Antarctic region. They seemed to form an endless procession across the horizon, their fantastic shapes resembling sculptured forms. Through the morning's light mist, I stared at those marvelous creations of nature. On rare moments when the sun broke through and shone upon them, Sverre and I gazed in awe at their enchanting beauty. The light fell softly in the smoking haze until the sides of the bergs glittered like cliffs of bright marble.

As the mist diminished, from our height we spotted penguins, swimming deep into the water. Those on deck could see them only when they surfaced or jumped onto the pack ice. I never got tired of their graceful and playful antics. Their presence helped the time pass more rapidly.

The *City*'s wooden bow, three feet thick, pushed through the broken pack ice. Under Sverre's commands, the helmsman steered the ship toward the black spots that indicated clear water.

Occasionally, the pack ice closed in. Our ship, although locked in the ice for many hours, went under power when the currents or wind released pressure on the ice. The power forced the ice to spread apart so we could move forward, seeking small, weak spaces in the pack. The ship went in a southerly direction, zigzagging from lead to lead.

We progressed slowly. In the past, the dangerous and unpredictable packs had kept other would-be explorers from reaching land. They rightly feared getting trapped by the ice and would not chance going farther. Few ships had gone into this pack ice before us. As we moved onward all of us on board sensed the danger every minute. Had we been caught in the ice, we might have had to abandon ship and go afloat in our lifeboats. Such a catastrophe had happened to others.

We inched our way forward — and it seemed like inchward progress. Thirty-two days elapsed before the ship reached our destination.

———————◆———————

My first view of the Ross Ice Barrier was of the magnificent ice cliffs that stood guard over the continent as if warning all intruders. Looming in front of us, the cliffs extended vertically as high as two hundred feet. We couldn't land there, so the ship moved eastward toward the Bay of Whales.

Byrd selected the Bay of Whales in the Ross Sea for two reasons. First, he believed it would provide the best conditions for his flight over the South Pole. Second, he wanted us to move around the yet-unexplored areas that surrounded the bay. The Bay of Whales was also the point nearest to the South Pole that ships could reach; it was fifty miles closer than the modern base at McMurdo Sound.

We would land in the same area where Amundsen built his camp, Framheim, in 1910. A member of our expedition, Martin Ronne, had reached Antarctica with Amundsen in 1910. Although he wanted to find the old camp as much as any of us, he did not have any landmarks. The ever-changing ice forms disoriented him, and he could never offer us any precise locations.

We never found Framheim, and it would have been surprising if we had. Falling and blowing snows had had sixteen years to bury the site that Amundsen abandoned in 1912. Soundings confirmed Byrd's theory that when the ice froze each year, it accumulated an additional two feet above the water in the low spots and six in the highest.

We sighted the Ross Barrier on December 24, 1928, and prepared to land on the ice on Christmas Day. Knowing how ships pulled into a landing, I figured that I would get ready to jump onto the ice ahead of the others. I assumed the skipper would guide the ship as close as possible to the ice, take a sharp left turn, and put the starboard side up against the ice. Then we could go down a ladder or jump over the side.

Normally the bowsprit, which extended sixty-five feet in front of the bow, swings over the land just as the vessel makes its hard left turn. By hanging under the tip of the bowsprit, I figured I could drop onto the ice, run over to the side of the ship, and welcome Byrd and his party ashore.

I hid under the bowsprit to make this unscheduled landing; the skipper turned, however, before the bowsprit went over the ice. I considered this an unorthodox landing and a personal affront because that didn't put me over the ice first.

Having failed to make my dramatic landing, I ran down the starboard side next to the gunwale. I wasn't alone in my desire to be first. Most of the men wanted to be number one, and we had a joyous competition over it. As it turned out, I was tenth.

After a few minutes of celebration, I stood aside from the others, staring at the Ross Sea. It appeared — deceptively — as smooth as a pond. We were in a narrow harbor, squeezed between sheer cliffs that rose a hundred feet in places. I breathed deeply, aware of the purity of the air. My fingers dug through my heavy clothes until they touched Father's watch. That gesture made me feel as if he shared the joyousness of the moment with me.

We had arrived at last. It had taken fifteen months from the time I first read the words "Byrd to the South Pole." We had landed on the unexplored continent, 13,323 nautical miles from Boston. Now we were ready for the real adventure.

———————◆———————

The first thing Byrd wanted to do was select the site for our future home. Long before, he had decided to name it Little America. A careful man, he wanted to choose the site personally and to be certain it rested on solid barrier ice — a place that wouldn't break off and float us northward on an Antarctic iceberg.

Byrd walked toward me and said, characteristically terse, "Vaughan, hitch up a team."

"Yes, sir, Commander."

"You're going with me."

"Yes, sir!"

I wonder if anyone can comprehend the excitement I felt that day. I was to be the first in our party to drive a team of dogs on the Antarctic continent. Byrd had asked *me*.

As I look backward, I can imagine the jealousy that must have inflamed Walden. Properly, he should have been the man to drive Byrd to the initial site. That had been his original position. But as far back as our days at Wonalancet, his indecisiveness and uncertainty had spoiled his opportunities for recognition.

In all honesty, I didn't give much thought then to how Walden must have felt. I was having the time of my life. It was like having the Harvard football coach yell for me to play in the big game against Yale in place of a first-string player.

I was first in going across the ice with a team. In one sense, we were all firsts because we were the first Americans to set foot on Antarctica.

When we started off, I became conscious of the wind whisking across the frozen ice. With no trees or structures to lessen its impact, the wind acted like a giant broom, sweeping the ground fairly level, leaving it with the hardness of concrete.

Although we planned to go only a short distance, in the polar regions everyone went prepared for the worst. We took along our sleeping bags, tents, food, and Byrd's navigational instruments. Byrd sat on the sled, and I rode behind or dogtrotted when necessary. Bernt Balchen and Sverre Strom, our Norwegian advance party, skied half a mile in front of us.

We quickly learned we could not trust our eyes in the Antarctic. We moved along smoothly and suddenly hit a ridge. We sighted a mountain of snow miles away only to discover it was a mere hill twenty yards in front of us. I saw a ridge only a short distance ahead that turned out to be miles farther.

Unable to tell the difference between night and day by the sun, we used the military twenty-four-hour periods instead of two twelve-hour segments. At this season, Antarctica was in its white night, when the sun doesn't set for three months.

After an hour Balchen and Strom encountered a pressure ridge and came back to report. A pressure ridge occurs when the ice is pushed by the winds and the sea against the harder inner ice. It's like the old dilemma of being caught between a rock and a hard place. The ice caught in the middle goes upward. This particular pressure ridge measured fifteen feet at its lowest point.

Both Strom and Balchen took off their skis to help my dog team over the ridge. One pulled the dogs while the other joined me in pushing. Once over, we tramped southward for a gradual climb from the bay ice onto the Ross Ice Barrier.

At that point everything looked white. The horizon blended into the sky so perfectly that I could hardly tell where the ice ended and the sky began. It was an eerie feeling. As I stared all around, I recalled one of those little paperweights that create snowstorms when you shake them. We had no snow, but for a few minutes I felt that we were miniatures in the same kind of enclosure.

Yet I felt an exhilaration, too. "I'm here! We're walking on land that no other American has ever touched before!"

Geologically, glacier ice is considered land. The greatest ice mass in the world covers this continent, allowing only the highest peaks to emerge. Not until months later did we see bare rock, usually lava stone, jutting out of the ground. When we spotted rocks, we could not have been more delighted had we seen a vast field of soft mown grass.

Although I never lost my excitement on that first outing, after a while the landscape took on a sameness. I had nothing to look at except my dogs and the men on skis as they lurched onward. To remain alert, I kept close watch to be sure the dogs continued forward and didn't get twisted in their harnesses or wander off the trail made for us by the two skiers. We had to be careful because at times their skis left no marks in the crusty snow.

Delighted to be moving and wide awake, I was eager for Byrd to claim a spot as Little America, our home for the next year. Since our dogs and sleds would transport all of the equipment and provisions, the farther we went from the two ships, the longer each trip for us. Consequently, I wanted to stop as soon as possible.

Finally the two skiers did stop and waited until my sled caught up. Balchen gestured. "Commander," he said, "how is this for a possibility? What do you think?"

Byrd got out of the sled and walked around in a small circle, silently evaluating the site. He turned to the other two men. After some discussion in which I had no part, Byrd decided to look a little farther. The barrier had gentle undulations of about two hundred feet from crest to crest. He needed a big ridge area so that the radio towers would be as high as possible.

I knew generally what we were looking for. Large ice masses frequently broke off from the reef and floated north as huge, flat, rectangular icebergs. (We have a record of one being more than a hundred miles long.)

Byrd got back onto the sled. He turned to me and said, "I don't want to wake up some morning and find Little America floating northward."

A bright, highly energetic man, Byrd never asked any of us to do anything he was not willing to do himself. He was also cautious and refused to take unwarranted risks with human lives. "A little farther, I think," he said as we mushed forward.

Another few minutes and we stopped again. Balchen and Strom skied back to the sled. Byrd and they agreed that this site was an excellent choice.

I finally heard the words I had waited for: "We'll set up Little America here!"

As our first task, Byrd ordered us to do something that remains one of my special memories. I unpacked two shovels from the sled. Byrd took one and handed Balchen the other. They started to dig. Then Strom and I took turns. We all wanted to be part of the momentous occasion. From the ice we cut out chunks roughly a cubic foot in size. We piled them one on top of another until they stood six feet high. Byrd then unfurled an American flag. Using a ski pole as a mast, he hoisted the colors.

"Shipmates," said the commander, with his eyes glowing, "today,

December 27, 1928, I name this Little America. May this flag wave here forever!"

Byrd had reached the Antarctic, the fulfillment of a three-year dream. Can I ever forget the change in his normally unemotional features and gestures as he spoke? My own heart beat rapidly, and as we stood in momentary silence, the harsh wind ripping at the flag, I wanted to cry from the joyousness of the occasion. I felt proud to be an American and honored to take part in the Byrd expedition. I was sure that never again would I experience such feelings of pride and utter joy.

The faces of Balchen and Strom, who later became naturalized Americans, glowed with the same heartfelt pride. I wondered whether they thought about their countryman, Roald Amundsen, who had disappeared only months before on a dangerous rescue flight in the North Atlantic. He had been the first conqueror of the South Pole.

I remember thinking, here we are, two Americans and two Norwegians, carrying on the work started by Amundsen. I wish I could have preserved those moments forever.

Having no more time for ceremonies, we went to work, laboring side by side. Rank forgotten, each man assisted in setting up two colored, dome-shaped tents. Strom and Balchen would share one, and I slept with Byrd in the other.

About that time, Arthur Walden and Carl Petersen arrived, having followed our tracks. They came to set up the communications system, and their sled carried radio equipment. We pitched in to erect a set of guy wires for the radio antenna. Immediately, Petersen attempted contact with the *City of New York*. His face registered both relief and pleasure with the response, "All is well."

With our location selected and contact made with the *City*, we were ready for our evening meal. All of us cooperated in cooking a supper of hoosh. Our version of this trail soup was made from pemmican. Not for the fastidious, pemmican is greasy and rich, made primarily from meat with indigestible parts removed and a thick stock added. Using Amundsen's formula, a Copenhagen firm had packed the product into boxes of twenty-five pounds each and sent it to the United States for the Byrd expedition. The hoosh tasted like a fatty, thick pea soup; adding crackers improved the taste somewhat. (We all learned to love the concoction.) After dinner we made hot chocolate.

Having had a busy day, everyone was tired. Walden and I didn't even take the dogs out of their harnesses. Not being harness chewers, they were safe for the night. After feeding our dogs, I joined Byrd in the tent. He was already in his sleeping bag, and I crawled into mine. Byrd must have thanked God for safety and our progress so far. I know I did.

With nothing more than a good-night to each other, we fell asleep.

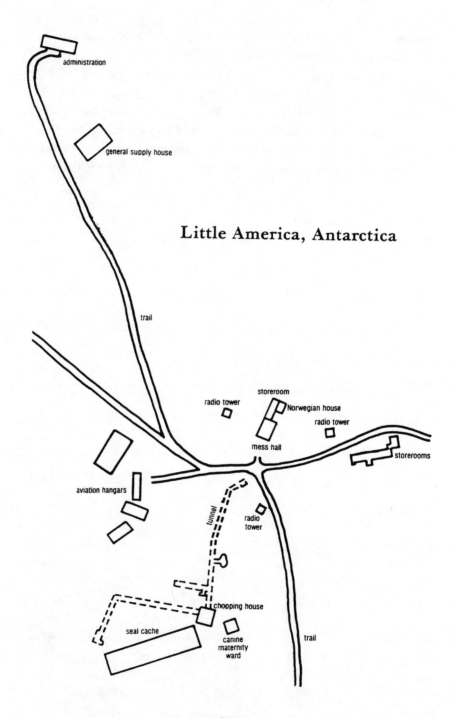

Little America, Antarctica

administration

general supply house

trail

radio tower

storeroom

Norwegian house

radio tower

mess hall

storerooms

aviation hangars

tunnel

radio tower

chopping house

seal cache

canine maternity ward

trail

The Long Hauls

When we returned to the ship the next morning, men were standing on deck waiting for us. Some rushed across the ice as soon as we came close, greeting us with shouts and hundreds of questions.

During the time we were gone, the men had not been idle. They had unloaded the other dog teams and begun stacking equipment on the ice, waiting for the signal to load our sleds for the trip to Little America.

First, however, the advance party sat down to a hot meal. Then we joined in unloading the ship. Every man in the expedition put in long hours of grueling work from that moment on. Until the long winter came, we would never have enough sleep and we would always feel tired. Yet I never heard a man complain.

We four dog drivers—Walden, Goodale, Crockett, and I—each taught a volunteer from the ship's crew to drive dogs. A Newfoundlander named Jack Bursey had some experience driving dogs, so he joined us, and he also taught a volunteer. Byrd reassigned them as our assistants. The new drivers learned quickly, and within a week each volunteer had become an independent driver. We now had ten drivers, and we needed every one of them.

Byrd had calculated that it would take three months to unload the *City of New York* and the *Eleanor Bolling* and set up our base at Little America. Until the builders could construct permanent housing on the site, we dog drivers, who spent the nights at Little America after delivering the second load of the day, slept in tents.

"See?" I said to Goodale and Crockett. "Sleeping in Walden's open gazebo last winter was good practice for us. This will be just like Wonalancet — only better!"

Also living in tents at Little America were the three builders. They worked with amazing speed and skill, setting up the buildings as fast as we brought them their materials. The complex was designed to be as functional yet comfortable as possible for the forty-two men who would spend the long night there — six months without sun.

The builders first dug a hole for the main house, which measured forty by thirty-two feet. It would be divided into mess hall, sleeping quarters, office, and everything else we needed. Later they constructed smaller buildings from packing crates. Byrd shared one hut with a dozen scientists. Although important to the expedition, the drivers were at the bottom of the list, so we slept in the last two buildings constructed.

While men were digging a foundation, our sleds continued to bring the materials. Byrd's people had planned prefabricated structures with portable panels bolted to each other, a forerunner of the prefab house. They designed two-by-eight planking that went underneath the house and on which they laid the floor. The wood panels came to us already insulated. We carried the roof in sections.

Eventually the builders erected three radio towers, each rising sixty-five feet and anchored five feet into the snow. The radio signals went primarily to the ship, with whom we made contact each day. Russell Owen, a reporter for the *New York Times,* needed the radio to send daily messages to his paper. When no significant events took place, he reported on the lifestyle, habits, and personalities of the members. (He later received the prestigious Pulitzer Prize for reporting the best story of 1929–1930.)

Every morning at six o'clock we drivers awakened, drank one or two cups of coffee, slipped into our heavy clothes and parkas, roused and harnessed our dogs to the twenty sleds, and set out for the ship. We transported every item to Little America by sled, providing the vital link between the two places.

A crew of workers chopped down the pressure ridges so that they were fairly smooth to go across, although in one place the trail still took a sudden upward movement followed by an immediate descent. The nine miles from camp to ship took us one hour and thirty minutes; the return trip, with a full load, was about four hours if all went well.

This going back and forth wore us down physically, but we kept going. None of us ever seemed to get enough sleep. We did figure out one way to get a little more rest, though: after unloading at Little America, we stretched out on the empty sleds and let the dogs pull us back to the ship. They knew the trail and were eager for the food and rest that awaited them there. We were so tired, we slept soundly the whole way, even when the dogs crossed over the pressure ridges. Only when the sleds came to a stop did we wake up.

The loading crew turned our teams around so that they were headed back to Little America and began loading the sleds for the next trip. Each team hauled two sleds in tandem, with about sixty percent of the weight on the front sled.

While the sleds were being loaded and the dogs were being fed, we headed below, where George "Gummy" Tennant, the expedition's cook, had an immense breakfast waiting for us: bacon, powdered eggs, sausage, butter, and fresh bread, all preceded by a big bowl of hot oatmeal. Sometimes he surprised us with doughnuts, fried bread, or pancakes. We always had a dish of fresh penguin, whale, or seal meat on the table. I didn't care what he laid out for us; I liked everything—even the whale's eye that Gummy served as a joke.

Breakfast over, we went over the side and lashed the loads ourselves. Because the movement on the ice often loosened the ropes, we had to know exactly how to tighten the lashings without undoing everything, and we didn't want to waste time on the journey.

After completing our first load, which took the entire morning, we ate a midday meal at Little America. In the afternoon, still tired, we slept on the way back to the ship and repeated the morning operation.

For the two daily runs between ship and camp we dogtrotted eighteen miles. Occasionally Byrd would ask us to make an extra trip. None of us refused, although it meant we would run twenty-seven miles that day, and the dogs, twice that.

We hauled six hundred fifty tons altogether. Byrd stayed at shipside and decided which items took priority. He wanted Little America built as quickly as possible, so we freighted essential materials first. Laurence McKinley Gould, our geologist and second in command, supervised activities at camp.

Being the great leader he was, Byrd stirred up a little healthy competition among the dog teams. Alongside the ship, he erected a blackboard with the names of all ten drivers. Next to each driver's name was the total weight his sleds had carried the day before, followed by his grand total. The ship's crew weighed each item before they put it on the sleds.

Every team wanted to be the one that had carried the most, so we kept trying to haul heavier and heavier loads. One driver who wanted to be on the top of the list snuck out of camp one night and made an extra trip. This competition almost killed us, but we got the job done. The maximum load for the biggest dogs was two thousand pounds, and the average was about sixteen hundred. We could carry the maximum load only when the sun was near the horizon and the trail was icy and fast. By noon, when the sun was strongest, the trail had usually softened, making the hauling more difficult.

We used nine dogs to a team. The five junior drivers with smaller dogs learned fast. Within a week they could carry twelve hundred to fifteen hundred pounds a trip. As they became more adept and familiar with the problems, they nearly equaled the weights carried by the more experienced. Soon all of us hauled the maximum weight for the size of the dogs every trip. The loads were so heavy that we mushers could never ride our sleds to Little America and had to dogtrot alongside.

The big pressure ridge, which shifted almost every day, gave us the one spot of trouble. Two teams had to work together there. We unhitched the second sled on each team and helped each other pull the first sleds over the ridge. We then returned for the second sleds. After pulling them over the ridge, we rehitched and continued. One time I lost my dogs while moving back over the pressure ridge to pick up the dropped load. The dogs ran back to Little America without me. I walked the remaining three miles to camp, collected the animals, rehitched them to a spare sled, and retrieved my load.

Seals and penguins wandering nearby made the operation especially tricky because the dogs welcomed any distraction from the monotonous pulling. The crack of a whip and an oath quickly reminded them of their duty.

---◆---

The captains of the *City* and the *Bolling,* always aware of the danger of the pack ice, had to change their positions regularly. Once they had to move several miles away because of the movement of an iceberg. That meant more work for us.

On January 24, 1929, the one day that the temperature rose above freezing, the snow turned soft. Our sleds sank lower and lower. The loading crew became concerned and began checking the ice at the loading sites, making sure it was thick enough to support both us and the sleds. No one, however, considered the potential danger posed by accumulations of soot and coal dust spewed out by the ships' engines. This waste material absorbed rather than reflected the sun's rays, and the several layers of warmed soot and coal were rotting the ice through. We thought we were working in soft, loose snow over a solid footing, but underneath, the soot was cutting all the way through to the water.

The section of ice on which I stood suddenly gave way, dropping me into the freezing water. Because I was so heavily dressed, I couldn't possibly have pulled myself back up onto the ice. Fortunately, Eddie Goodale was nearby. Grabbing my arms, he hauled me to safety.

---◆---

One time the Newfoundlander, Jack Bursey, tipped into a crack in the ice as he was heading to Little America with a full load. He saved the entire load by throwing himself in front of the runners, jerking his body across the narrow crevasse and wedging himself between the first sled and the far side of the hole. Had that front sled weighed more, it would have pulled Bursey, his dogs, and the second sled into the water and an icy death. As it was, he was in a most precarious position.

Frightened, he yelled to his companion driver, who continued with his own team, thinking Bursey was just shouting at his dogs. Had it not been for an alert lookout on the *City,* who quickly sent a rescue team, Jack Bursey would have died from exposure. When rescued, he was in the early stages of hypothermia and could not have held on much longer.

From the first day, Byrd had ordered us to work together and stated that at least two dog teams must stay together on the trail. After giving the other driver a severe and well-deserved tongue-lashing, Byrd relieved him and assigned him to stay aboard the *City.*

It took us from December 27, 1928, until March 25, 1929 — three full months, just as Byrd had calculated — to carry the six hundred and fifty tons of material from the two ships. Two planes, a Fokker and a Fairchild, flew off the bay ice to Little America. But the third plane, a Ford trimotor and the heaviest load on the expedition, was to go overland. It was so wide, we didn't know how we were going to get it off the *City,* much less carry it across the ice. Then the ship's captain found a low place in the face of the Ross Ice Shelf. With the assistance of the *Bolling,* the crews used the booms of both vessels and lifted the plane onto the barrier, at a spot where there were no pressure ridges.

The plane was enormous and weighed an unbelievable amount. Byrd walked around it, paused several times, and then came over to me. "Vaughan, can you pull it with the dogs?"

"I don't know, sir," I said honestly, "but we'll certainly give it a try."

"Go to it," Byrd said as he walked off.

We hitched all ninety-seven dogs to one long hawser, one team in front of another. Mine was last and closest to the plane. We had a difficult time getting the plane moving because the skis had frozen to the barrier ice. We hadn't known that we could not leave a ski-equipped plane resting on the snow because the skis themselves freeze.

After an hour and a half of straining for both animals and men, the plane started to move slowly. We never did figure out how we got the load moving, but once it started, we sensed success. We yelled, the dogs pulled, and without daring to pause, we dragged the Ford trimotor all nine miles to camp.

———————◆———————

To house the dogs, we dug a semicircular ditch seven feet deep and three feet wide. Every four feet along the tunnel we hollowed out a place for a dog box in the snow wall. Across the top of the open tunnel we placed a roof of slabs of ice and hard snow. The wind blew loose snow over the roof, and within three days we could drive our dog teams safely over the covered tunnel.

For a supplement to the dog food we had brought from New Zealand, we used seal meat. The flesh of seals contains the combination of fat and protein that dogs need for extremely heavy work in frigid conditions. In water these mammals fear the killer whales. On land, however, they have no natural enemies, and they never tried to get away from me. I could walk up close enough to use my Colt .45 and kill many at a time.

The addition of seal meat to the dogs' diet produced an almost immediate reaction. Their coats became shiny; they seemed more healthy and proved it by working harder than ever. Such benefits, how-ever, came at a high cost to me, and I was soon to suffer considerable pain in their behalf. I knew little about seals except that they made the best food for the dogs. Through ignorance I brought upon myself a problem that could have killed me. Had Dr. Dana Coman, our medical officer, not been in our party, I likely would have died.

After completing a day's work of freighting, I set out to kill enough seals to last us the rest of the winter — one hundred sixty-five seals. While the other drivers and their teams worked hard to pull the carcasses into camp, where we stacked them like logs, I began skinning the seals,

51

taking out the innards, and cutting the carcasses into sections. I had dressed only the first dozen or so seals before Bernt Balchen stopped me.

"You do not need to do this much work," he said in his heavily accented English. "The dogs eat everything."

Glad for his advice, after that I did nothing more than cut the carcasses into chunks. We fed the dogs the entire body — meat, fat, bones, and intestines. It made less work. By then, however, it was too late.

I developed a bad chafe between my legs. It started with an irritating itch and grew progressively worse until it burned all the time. I applied an ointment, hoping the salve would take care of my problem. Instead, the chafed area spread down my legs until the burning became unbearable. Even liberal sprinklings of talcum powder didn't help; I just got worse.

After four days, I had to have relief. "Can you give me something for this chafing?" I asked Dr. Coman. "Something to dry it up?"

"Let's have a look at it," he said.

I pulled down my pants and underwear, and he carefully examined me. "A salve won't help," he said, shaking his head.

"But I've got to have relief!"

"Well, that's not the way to get it. You have a parasite that spreads through contact." He explained that the microscopic larva of the parasitic worm lodges and multiplies between the epidermis and the dermis. Apparently, when I was skinning and cleaning the seals and had their blood on my bare hands, the parasites attached themselves. When I urinated, the worms moved into the crotch area, multiplying so rapidly in number and size that Coman could actually see them.

"Lie down and I'll see what I can do," Coman said.

I lay on the table while he worked methodically, my fingers digging into my palms so that I wouldn't scream from the excruciating pain. As he pulled the worms out one by one with pointed forceps, I felt as if he were yanking out my intestines. Each extraction felt like a hot needle.

When he finished removing all the worms he could see, he covered the inflamed area between my legs with sheets of adhesive tape six inches wide extending around my legs. Taking off the adhesive tape each morning was almost as painful as having the worms extracted. The tape seemed to pull my skin from my body, despite the profuse use of alcohol to loosen it. And then it was time for another round of extractions.

By the time Coman covered me up again, I felt so weak that it seemed the sensible thing to go to bed for the rest of the day. But I believed I was as strong as any man on the ice, and I wouldn't allow anything like a parasite to sideline me.

Between the ship and Little America, I cried out loud and actually wept from the pain. No one could hear me, and it seemed to help to let out the pain through tears. Once, my misery was so intense that I slouched against the load and whimpered until Goodale's team behind me almost caught up. I faked fixing a loose line and pushed on. He never knew how badly I hurt.

I remember mumbling to myself that they might have to pick up my dead body on the trail, but they wouldn't find me voluntarily in the sick bay. I cursed my stubbornness and was tempted to give in fifty times. But because the doctor kept insisting that I quit, I was more determined than ever to prove to him I could do it.

He'd shake his head and say, "Okay, Vaughan, it's your body."

"If it gets so bad I can't run anymore, then I'll quit," I promised.

Goodale and Crockett, after seeing the inflamed area, urged me to take sick leave for at least one day.

"I'm able to do my work," I insisted. "I'll be all right."

They did help me by hauling chunks of frozen seal meat for my dogs and leaving it where I tethered my team for the night.

Fortunately, the worms clustered around my crotch and down the inside of my legs and did not spread farther. They seemed to feed on perspiration. Coman tried his best to keep me dry and clean. "Keep your pants open, Vaughan," he said. "That'll stop you from heating up so much."

We made a few jokes about it, but I knew he was right. As soon as I got on the trail, I opened my pants and let the air penetrate. This daily pulling out of worms and rebandaging went on for two weeks—the hardest, most painful two weeks of my life. But he eventually extracted all the parasites and I recovered.

Danger in the Night

Another problem remained, one that was just as serious but in a very different way: Arthur Walden. Vaguely aware of Walden's resentment before we left Wonalancet, on the ice I watched his jealousy grow and begin to show itself openly.

In New Hampshire we three Harvard fellows had stuck together. We firmly believed in working things out without asking for help. In the few instances when we did ask, Walden did not know what to do. We ended up figuring the solutions out for ourselves. After a few months he stopped discussing anything about dogs with the three of us, especially with me.

By the time we left America, we had tacitly agreed that Walden would take care of his own dogs and I would be in charge of the others. I never gave any orders to or about his dogs. He kept his Chinooks separate from the others and did whatever he wanted with them.

We musketeers were a cocky and independent trio. Walden, old enough to be our father, probably expected to remain our leader by virtue of his age and experience. By the time we landed at Antarctica, however, we figured we knew almost as much about dogs as he did.

Walden became aloof and spent most of his free time caring for his Chinooks. The breach widened. He spoke to us less and less.

One thing that added to his depression was the loss of his lead dog, Chinook. When brought to the ice, the dog was twelve years old and too weak for hard, continual labor. Walden used him for what he called a "shock troop" by throwing him in with his team when he hit a bad spot on the trail. Old Chinook would join with the younger dogs, working as if he were three years old. I believe Walden loved that dog more than he did any human being. He boasted that he never needed to give Chinook an order because the dog knew exactly what to do.

In late January, Chinook disappeared. Despite an intensive search, we never found him. Walden grieved over that animal. Several of us speculated that the dog, aware of his age, purposely wandered off to die. Until we left the ice, Walden never stopped grieving for and talking about his lost companion.

I wonder if, in his twisted and depressed thinking, he blamed me for stealing or killing his dog. No dog man would ever do such a thing, but by that time Walden wasn't always thinking rationally.

Walden had trained a Norwegian named Chris Braathen as his assistant dog driver. After Braathen became an independent driver, Walden remained friendly with him, and they lived in a house with two other Norwegians. He tended to stay away from the Americans and associated with just the people from his house.

The lengthening darkness on the ice seemed to worsen Walden's depression. He grew intensely lonesome. He missed being at home and talked incessantly about his wife and Wonalancet and the beauty of New Hampshire. Expressing utter hatred for life at Little America, he grumbled about the monotony of the landscape and the constantly changing weather.

Walden had never been isolated like this before. By nature, he was gregarious and active. He enjoyed a well-earned reputation in New Hampshire for knowing more about mushing dogs than anybody else. The locals knew he had carried mail and freight across Alaska by dog sled. They looked up to him as a minor hero and master of dog driving. Drawing from an endless number of stories about his activities in Alaska, he spun his yarns well; everybody, including the three musketeers, liked listening to them.

When we reached Antarctica, however, Walden was no longer the star. After a few weeks no one cared much about his Alaskan stories. As far as the dogs were concerned, I had outshone him because of my high energy and initiative. I loved adventure and hated to think I might miss out on one. Walden could have volunteered for more responsibility, but he never did. So in time, the men recognized that I had taken his place as the man in charge of the dogs.

Byrd often asked me to do things that should have been Walden's task, such as being the driver on the trip to set the location for Little America. When he wanted to know about the general condition of the animals, their food supply, or their shelter, he asked me. Byrd didn't intentionally try to hurt Walden. Had he disliked him, Byrd was the kind of leader who would have ordered him to board the ship and return to New Zealand.

Although Walden began to withdraw and become sullen toward us, he still continued to do his job well during the unloading period. Only after we stopped our demanding work and he had more time to brood did he become worse. He showed obvious hostility toward me. Too bad, I thought, but that happens sometimes. I was too busy having the time of my life to care. Despite the exhausting work, and even later when we had plenty of time, I could hardly wait for each morning to come. The expedition was everything I had ever hoped it would be.

In April we lost the sun. Now only pale moonlight lightened the twenty-four hours of darkness. The long night of continued and total darkness affects people differently. Walden himself admitted that. Russell Owen, the journalist among us who wrote a book on his return, quoted the "old Alaskan Dog Driver" as saying, "This place makes good men better and bad men worse."

Owen, I guess, didn't want to embarrass anyone by using our names. But it was clear whom he meant when he wrote in his diary,

> The Dog Driver always thinks in terms of Alaska and maintains
> that this is the most uninteresting experience he has ever known.

Even the sledging here is monotonous, he says, because it is so
smooth and easy going. He longs for the woods, with the snow on
them, difficult trails through the underbrush, the howl of wolves at
night, and beans and bacon for food. The only decent trail ration
he can imagine is beans. . . . His anger is a dangerous thing . . .

Walden's depression deepened. He lost all semblance of his former
outgoing personality. He turned morose and acted rudely toward everyone. No matter how hard Crockett and Goodale tried to engage him in
conversation, monosyllabic answers were the best they received. After a
few weeks, he refused to speak to me.

It became embarrassing to be near him at mealtimes. For a while he
alternated between totally ignoring me and staring at me while I ate. I
did my best to avoid him. When I saw him go into the mess hall for
meals, I stayed out with the dogs or found another task to do until he
finished.

Except for meals, Walden spent his time in the Norwegian house.
As the winter progressed, we all stayed indoors most of the time. We
drivers relieved the monotony by going out to the dog tunnels and caring
for our dogs. Reading occupied a lot of hours. When the weather was
tolerable, we took walks down to the bay ice.

Then Byrd announced that Goodale, Crockett, and I would go out
with Larry Gould's geological party when the sun came back to Antarctica. This assignment gave us a lot of preparatory work that demanded
many hours each day. During the ninety days of freighting we had worn
out our harnesses. Now we busily repaired them. With the skilled help of
Bernt Balchen and Sverre Strom we learned to fix broken sleds. We
made gloves, patched harnesses, repaired tents, packed food, and made
sure we had everything ready for the trail when Byrd gave us the signal. I
didn't think about it then, but Walden's not being assigned to the survey
trip must have enraged and humiliated him.

Byrd also assigned me to work out the logistics for the geological
expedition. I had to decide what we needed in food and equipment based
on an expected round trip of fifteen hundred miles for six men and forty-
six dogs. We would face temperatures of minus forty degrees when we

started with our heaviest loads. Our four-inch-wide wooden runners would drag hard at that temperature. My first calculations, based on providing the maximum amount of supplies, totaled more weight than we could possibly carry on our sleds.

When I showed Byrd, he said, "Pare down the figures."

I returned to my worksheets and began figuring it out so that we wouldn't overload our sleds and yet would have sufficient supplies for three months. The busier I was, however, the more Walden seemed to smolder.

When forty-two men live in an isolated area in total darkness for half a year, strains show. True character emerges, and we have less control over our tempers. Before long, the others recognized Walden's strange behavior. More than one man commented on his staring, which he directed at me for as long as an hour at a time. I didn't say much in response, but I read hatred in his unblinking eyes.

Hoping we could get past this strange alienation, I tried various approaches: ignoring him, joking with him, making statements to elicit simple responses. He would never answer or even indicate that he had heard me.

We still had months of darkness ahead of us, and none of us could leave. The ships had returned to New Zealand. Things could only worsen. And they did.

I began to feel nervous about being in the same room with a man who would not speak to me or acknowledge my presence. It was hard enough to be shut up in a room filled with friendly men, twenty-four hours a day.

As I reflected on our deteriorating relationship, I felt some concern. I had earned my way into the expedition. Byrd liked my work and that of my two Harvard friends. I hadn't purposely tried to take over, but neither did I give an inch. In the early days at Wonalancet, Walden had been the top authority, and we had learned a lot from him. But I wouldn't bow to him now because he had lost his authority. I saw no reason to offer any apology or to go out of my way to bring peace. He had backed off; he had stopped talking; he gave me the sullen stares. I did feel sorry for him and wished the situation were different.

By constantly volunteering, I soon had a wider range of experience on the ice than Walden. In my eagerness to know everything about this strange land, I worked hard, asked questions, and learned fast. We were all doing things that none of us had ever done before. I went to Antarctica as green as Walden, but I soon had an edge because I was physically stronger and younger, and I took the initiative.

One day, Braathen motioned for me to go outside with him. Curious, I followed. He walked behind the building, out of sight of the other men.

"I have come to warn you," the Norwegian said, pronouncing each word distinctly.

"About what?"

"Walden. He is out to get you."

"I know he doesn't like — "

"No. It is now different. He carries a gun."

"Are you sure?" I could hardly believe that Walden had gotten that bad.

"We watch him every day," Braathen said. "He is planning to shoot you."

"Why the hell don't you take the gun away from him? There must be six of you in there from time to time."

"No, no." He shook his head. "Doing that might upset him more. Who knows what he might do if we forced the gun away from him."

"Who knows what he'll do if you don't grab the damn gun!"

"No. It is better that we wait."

"You're afraid of what he might do to the six of you? So I'm supposed to walk around here, knowing he's got a loaded gun, that he hates me and might try to shoot me?" Braathen's reasoning sounded as crazy to me as Walden's bizarre behavior. "You expect me to go on living normally while I wait for you to get around to disarming him?"

"He is acting strange," Braathen said.

"I know that!"

"Be patient and stay alert," Braathen said. "We are keeping our eyes on him. We shall take the gun from him when we can."

"I hope you'll work fast. It takes only two seconds to pull out a gun and fire it."

"We are trying to talk him out of carrying it. So our word to you is to be awake at all times." He walked back into the mess hall.

In a closed environment like ours, the word spread quickly through whispers and confidential conversations that Walden was packing a gun. That bit of news made the others who hadn't known the severity of the situation realize just how bad it had become. The Norwegians particularly understood: When Walden first bunked with them, he had tried to turn them against me. Although not grasping everything he said, they had treated me with reserve. Walden had finally said to Braathen, "I can't stand this any longer." He had waved the gun around, making wild threats about what he would do to me. As soon as he had quieted Walden, Braathen called me aside to warn me. From then on, the Norwegians kept me informed, hoping to settle things peacefully and not involve the entire camp.

I owned a gun, the Colt .45 I used to kill seals. After considering the matter, however, I decided I wouldn't arm myself. I didn't want to be involved in some kind of old-fashioned, Wild West shoot-out. I would have to figure out another strategy.

The only place we all assembled every day was in the mess hall. I was reasonably sure he wouldn't try to shoot me in front of anybody else. If he decided to use the gun, he would do it when he found me alone.

As I lay sleepless in bed, trying to think how to save my skin, a hollow sensation struck the pit of my stomach. I was scared. No one had ever wanted to kill me before. I thought, I have come all the way down to Antarctica and I will never see my mother again.

I decided that my safety lay in staying away from Walden and never allowing him to be alone with me. But what about nights? Even though I bunked with four other men, he could sneak in and find me zipped inside my sleeping bag, almost defenseless. If Walden came after me then, he wouldn't even need a gun; his hands would be enough.

I determined that I wouldn't get caught in bed. Slipping off my upper bunk, I crept outside. I would sleep out-of-doors. Only a few yards beyond the radio towers were endless miles into which I could disappear. Searching for me would be like hunting a minnow in an ocean. With a pup tent under my arm and dragging a broken sled, I paced off one hundred steps and looked around. The crescent moon was new, but it gave a slight form to the drifts near the camp. I shook my head. "Not far enough."

I counted out another fifty paces. At this distance I could still see the towers, but Walden would not be able to find me. Feeling secure, I pitched my tent and crawled inside.

Each night I sneaked out and walked a circuitous route for twenty minutes—far enough away so that Walden would have a hard time finding me if he decided to track me down. Goodale and Crockett knew approximately where I was, even though I moved the tent every other night. Dragging a snowshoe behind me covered my footprints. Occasionally, weather conditions made it difficult to erect a tent, but I got used to putting it up. By digging into the snow about a foot, I made a firm foundation to anchor the tent. I shoveled snow around the base to keep the winds from taking the whole structure and brought a broken sled inside for added weight.

During the day the sled held the tent down against the relentless winds. Each night I walked over, changed my socks, made sure my feet were dry, and wriggled into my sleeping bag. I soon settled into a comfortable position.

Ten days after warning me, the Norwegians took the gun away from Walden. With that lethal weapon gone, I relaxed somewhat but still worried he might decide to kill me; I continued to hide out and sleep in my tent for two months. Although temperatures at night usually dropped to forty below, I stayed fairly warm. Our meteorologist quoted our lowest temperature as minus seventy-three. On extremely cold nights when I couldn't sleep, I went into the mess hall, sat down at a table, and read by the light of a kerosene lamp. Before morning I had usually dozed off. The eighteen men sleeping there gave me a feeling of security.

Lying alone, isolated from everyone else, I was still afraid. I would awaken with a start at any unusual noise, and I never walked a straight line to or from my tent. If Walden ever did try to find me, I figured, the myriad footprints around the camp made by the other men would confuse him.

My going out became routine, but I never stopped being scared. I observed Walden's strange behavior throughout the day and never allowed myself to forget that he had turned into a dangerous man.

Life in Camp

Byrd didn't know about Walden—frankly, it never occurred to me to trouble him with my problems—but he couldn't help but notice Ashley "Mac" McKinley. A close friend of Byrd's before the expedition, he was the official expedition photographer, constantly working when we had light. After the sun disappeared in April, McKinley had nothing to do until it reappeared. In November he would fly over the Pole with Byrd to take on the major project of photographing the topography.

Inactivity on the ice can be hard on anyone, but McKinley was a former Army man accustomed to staying active, and too much free time made him think about home. He began to feel homesick for his wife, Grace. Normally, he was quiet and friendly, but having nothing to do, Mac detached himself from the rest of us and became a loner. Never much of a talker, he spoke less and less. Even if we hadn't noticed that, we couldn't ignore the more serious sign of his depression: the increasing number of hours he slept.

Mac got so depressed that he slept nearly twenty hours at a time. He got up for lunch, ate his food indifferently, went back to his bed, and didn't get up again until lunchtime the next day. He seemed to drag himself, as if every gesture cost him the maximum effort. When Mac did talk, his conversation centered on his beloved wife and home, good food, and the conveniences of life in America. His voice sounded increasingly mournful.

Most of us learned quickly the one rule about home: Don't talk about it nostalgically. Reliving and relating pleasant experiences back in the States only deepened our sense of longing, as it did in McKinley's case.

The commander saw what was happening. He called McKinley aside, and the two men talked quietly in Byrd's quarters. I'm reporting the conversation that McKinley himself told me.

"Mac," Byrd said, "I've got a real problem on my hands, and I don't know how to handle it. It's an important mission that requires the right man. Frankly, I don't know whom to ask."

"What kind of job is it?"

Byrd lowered his voice and said, "I can't have just any man do this job. Secrecy is absolutely essential."

"You know you can trust me."

"I wouldn't be talking to you like this if I didn't have total confidence in you, Mac. You see, I have something important that I must hide in the barrier. It must be hidden so deep in the ice that no one will know and no one can find it by accident."

After Byrd talked along that line, never defining the "something," he said, "Mac, I trust you and I need your help. Will you help me find somebody for this important mission? It must be someone who can do the job and keep it an absolute secret."

"Have you asked Gould?" McKinley said. Officially, Larry Gould was second in command.

"No, I haven't talked to him yet. I'll do that this afternoon, but I thought I'd speak to you about it first. I must stress, Mac, that I don't want anybody to know that this job is being done."

McKinley finally took the bait. "Commander, if you want, I'd like to do the job for you. I can keep anything a secret. Besides, I'm not very busy."

66

"Gee, Mac," Byrd said, "that would be splendid. Would you really do it? I don't want you to feel you have to do this."

"I'd be glad to do it for you, Commander," he said. "I'd really like to."

Within an hour Ashley McKinley's important mission began. From outside the window of Byrd's quarters he started digging a long tunnel six feet high and three feet wide, three feet under the surface — deep enough that no one walking on the top would break through. Mac worked industriously, never speaking to anyone, trying to be as inconspicuous as possible. He used one of our small sleds to haul out the snow. Making sure no one was watching, he scattered it downwind, careful not to make a pile anywhere. That way, no one suspected what was going on. Every day Byrd went out, and speaking in hushed tones, he commended McKinley's efforts and then inspected the tunnel.

A miracle took place before our eyes. McKinley stopped being morose. He got up every morning, ate three meals a day, worked all day, slept well at night, and stopped his maudlin talk about home. Before long Mac was joking with the rest of us, just like his old self. Somehow — and we didn't know how — he had become a human being again.

Byrd never told McKinley how he planned to use the tunnel. But he made sure he gave his friend every kind of encouragement to stay with the digging. When the sun finally returned, Byrd would say things like, "I need a lot more work done here, but I just can't spare you much longer, Mac. You're doing a splendid job."

He also reminded McKinley that he wanted everything set for their flight over the Pole. "You've got to get your cameras and film ready. You're working hard on this secret project, but I don't want it to interfere with your being prepared for the flight."

"Oh, no, sir," McKinley assured him. "I have everything ready now. So I can stay with this project a little longer."

"If you're absolutely certain —"

"Yes, sir, I am."

"All right, then," Byrd said. "Keep it up for a few more days, Mac."

So far as I know, Byrd never told anybody about Mac's important mission. I learned about the project only because I watched McKinley disappearing into his tunnel, where he stayed all day. And being curious about everything connected with the expedition, I asked, "Mac, what's going on?"

He put me off. "Oh, a little work for the commander."

"What kind of work?"

"Oh, nothing much." He walked away and returned to his chore.

I kept after Mac until he finally said he would tell me if I promised not to break secrecy. Naturally, I did promise (and I kept my word for many years). Listening to Mac's story, I couldn't figure out why Byrd would want such a long, deep tunnel. Or why he needed any tunnel at all. By continuing to watch McKinley work and observing the change that came over him, I began to understand. Byrd's ingenious plan made me admire our commander all the more.

Victor Czegka was Little America's shop man and an outstanding mechanical engineer. He had recently retired from the Marine Corps and must have been in his midfifties. I liked Victor very much, but he was the most hardheaded man I've ever known.

If anyone crossed him—no matter how slightly, no matter whether by intention or by accident—he would throw a temper tantrum. Words spewed out of his mouth. He'd throw whatever happened to be handy and drive the object of his wrath right out of his workshop. By the next day, however, his anger forgotten, Victor smiled at the world and life seemed normal again.

Victor Czegka treated his workshop like a priest's private altar. Going into his workshop was like visiting a model room because he had everything perfectly set up with spaces marked on the wall for saws, hammers, and other tools. He never put anything in the wrong spot or left a file carelessly on the workbench.

In his magnificently arranged workshop, Victor's prized possession was the steel lathe, used to turn steel and fashion tools when they broke. He used to boast that he could take any part of the plane Byrd would use to fly over the Pole and make a duplicate. Perhaps an exaggeration, but he was so superb at what he did that we didn't challenge him.

While unquestionably a genius in his field, Victor Czegka hated dog drivers. We seemed constantly to get in his way or to cause him undue work. If we broke a runner on the trail, Victor took the break as a personal affront, implying that we had planned it. He fixed every broken object we brought him, but amid grumbling and denouncing of dogs and dog drivers. I had only one run-in with Victor Czegka, and it was enough.

During our unloading of the ships, one day I returned to Little America with my dogs in harness just in time for lunch. As soon as I had eaten, I would have to go back on the trail to the ship for another load. On that particular day I was ravenously hungry and in a big hurry to eat. I saw Victor walking to the mess hall, and I knew he would be away from his shop for a while. Seeing no other likely place to tie the dogs, I took my team to his workshop. Since Victor wasn't working his lathe, I figured he wouldn't mind if I tied them to one leg of it.

That was a grave mistake.

I went in and ate lunch. Goodale involved me in a conversation, and I didn't notice when Victor left the mess hall, headed back to his shop. But I knew it a few moments later. I heard the most awful shouting, and then the high priest of the workshop burst into the mess hall, screaming unprintable words.

"Who left those dogs in my shop?" he bellowed. Everyone in the hall had stopped eating and fallen silent. No one even dared to look at Victor, he was so angry. Except me, of course.

"I did," I said with all innocence, wondering what my dogs could possibly have done that would enrage him like that. How could those weary animals have had the strength to damage a steel lathe?

He rushed across the room, thrust his contorted face into my own, and with his voice at its highest pitch and top volume, let the words fly. With hardly any pause for breath, he concluded his lengthy diatribe:

"Nobody ties anything to my lathe! Nobody gets close to my lathe! And nobody—especially dogs and dog drivers—touches my lathe! *Nobody!*"

He turned and left. I raced out behind him, certain he had unleashed the dogs (he had) and just as certain they had taken off (they hadn't). In fact, my team lay peacefully just where I had left them, unaware, I assume, that they had been untied.

From then on Victor marked us drivers as the lowest of the men on the ice, perhaps upon the earth's surface. I never repeated my mistake. Among ourselves we joked that the unpardonable sin was not to murder or steal but to tie our dogs to the leg of Victor's lathe.

For two days he glared at me every time we passed each òther. I finally decided that Victor Czegka just wasn't an animal lover.

Byrd's choice of location for Little America proved a good one because his subsequent expeditions were able to use the same buildings, as well as the supplies we left behind. At the time, however, we didn't know how solid the ice was, so Laurence Gould, the geologist, had Sverre Strom make weekly surveys to determine whether our camp was in any danger of breaking away on an Antarctic iceberg.

On one such survey, Chris Braathen and his dog team went along with Sverre, who was on skis, to keep him company. When they encountered a patch of freshly frozen, transparent saltwater ice between two areas of thick, old bay ice, Sverre carefully tested the new ice to be sure that they could safely cross. The ice measured five inches thick — strong enough to hold them.

As they started across, Sverre suddenly felt himself being pushed up from underneath. A killer whale, seeing the form above, thought it was a seal and crashed the ice, hoping the seal would flop in. Sverre knew immediately what was happening and skied hard, using his poles and his long stride as he tried to reach the safety of the opaque ice.

Chris, too, understood the peril, and holding on to his sled with a death grip, he yelled to Moose-Mouse, his leader. "Gee! Gee! Go on, gee!" The dog heard the panic in his master's voice and obeyed instantly. The team swung around to the right and, within seconds, pulled Chris out of danger.

But ten yards still lay between Sverre and safety. The dark form of the whale pursued him like a huge shadow. Again the ice shattered as the whale burst to the surface, smashing the five-inch crust as if it were nothing more than thin plate glass. With a frantic thrust of his ski poles, Sverre propelled himself onto thick ice, out of the whale's sight. As he turned around, he saw chunks of ice bobbing in a circle of black water, his ski tracks on either side of the hole. The whale had disappeared.

Radio came to the public in 1922 and by 1929 had reached many homes. Another decade would pass before a radio was in every house, but on the ice we had a marvelous radio connection provided by the *New York Times* station in Schenectady, which transmitted directly to us. It set a record for transmitting a sustained program the longest distance.

On Saturday nights we picked up a program filled with personal messages from our families. Some of the messages became sources of ongoing conversation and humor. One fellow, William C. Haines, tried to carry on a romance with two girls at the same time by radio. Haines worked it so that he received a message from the girls on alternate Saturdays. One of them would express her affection but always end with some hint about having heard the other girl's message the previous week. She would also indulge in a little gossip about her rival to discredit her.

Because of our isolation, every bit of news was good for days. We looked forward to our own messages but anticipated just as eagerly the latest installments of Haines's two-pronged romance. Naturally we kidded him about these two girls, but he took the ribbing well.

Not all the messages were fun; my father sent a sad piece of news. Gordon, my half-brother, already gravely ill from tuberculosis when I left home, died while I was at Little America. Although expected, the news still saddened me.

The most joyful message for me came when Western Electric invited Mother to travel from Boston to Schenectady and talk to me on the radio. It was a wonderful thing for the utility to do.

Mother had written her message and read it aloud. Her voice was clear, and I felt elated just to hear her speak. She must have practiced because she sounded like she was talking without the script. But because

I knew her so well, I picked up several hints that she was nervous. She told me all about my friends and family members and things of interest that they had done. Aware that others were listening, she thoughtfully tried to make most of her talk appeal to them as well.

We never knew whose voice we would hear. When Mother's unexpected message came over the loudspeaker, the excitement of hearing her was just too much for me. Tears filled my eyes and ran down my cheeks. I was the second-youngest member of the expedition, and the others seemed to understand. Even if they hadn't, it wouldn't have made any difference. The tears came without warning, and I couldn't have stopped them. At the moment, nothing mattered except listening to her voice.

───────◆───────

A month after we lost the sun at Little America, Byrd gave the man in charge of supplies an order: "I want you to issue every man a new shirt."

That order may not sound like much, but it produced a fantastic amount of excitement. I had not had a new item of clothing since leaving Wonalancet eight months earlier. We had been at Antarctica five months, working and living and sleeping in the same clothes.

Giving out the shirts was another example of Byrd's fine leadership. Before we left America, he had ordered that those shirts be made up for us individually, according to each man's size. Every one of us would have a good fit.

The supply officer brought out a wooden box, and we watched as he pried off the lid. We stared at the gray shirts, one hundred percent wool. They were the most beautiful clothes we could imagine. We didn't say much when we got our shirts. After all, we were rugged men who didn't get excited about something so simple. Naturally, no one put on the shirt that day. None of us wanted the others to know how deeply we tough, winter-hardened men were affected. The next morning, however, we all appeared at breakfast in our new shirts.

Then a strange thing happened: We caught colds. Every last one of us — without exception — caught cold that day. We sneezed, we coughed, our throats felt scratchy, and we complained about headaches.

Dr. Coman finally concluded that whoever packed our shirts must have had a terrible cold. That person must have sneezed while packing the shirts. The germs, trapped inside and kept in cold storage for months, were preserved and waiting for us. And they got us.

We began to take massive doses of vitamin C, and within a few days we threw off the effects of the cold. We were so delighted to have the new shirts, we decided they were worth the suffering.

Liquor was not part of our rations at Little America, as Byrd demanded sobriety of his men. On passing through the Panama Canal, however, the military hospital gave Byrd a fifty-five-gallon drum of pure alcohol for medicinal purposes. Although it was meant to be hidden, we all knew where it was, and some of us tapped it from time to time.

Toward the end of winter the barrel was tapped every night by a group of men who gathered to enjoy a few shots mixed with fruit juice.

After one of these nocturnal parties, one man was missing. His buddies went through the buildings, searching for him. They didn't dare enter the dog tunnels, however, for fear of being bitten, so they woke Goodale and Crockett. (As usual, I was not in my assigned bunk.) The two dog drivers dressed and proceeded to search the tunnels. The lost man was finally found, curled up and asleep in Ooli's crate. Ooli, one of my dogs, was tough and untrustworthy. I was always aware of the possibility he could turn vicious. But here he was, outside his dog house, lying in the snow, happy and comfortable as the guardian of the inebriated.

One evening there was a bit of punch left over from the night before, and Chip, our carpenter, finished it off. Feeling no pain, he went down the tunnel to the storeroom where the drum was kept.

To siphon the fluid, a dedicated drinker had to gently inhale through a soft rubber hose. As soon as he felt the liquid reach his fingers, some twenty inches from his mouth, he had to quickly put the end of the tube into a large pitcher to collect the alcohol.

On this evening, however, Chip inhaled too vigorously and wasn't quick enough. Alcohol flooded his mouth. At minus fifty-five degrees Fahrenheit, the liquid burned the inside of his mouth and throat so badly that Dr. Coman thought we would lose him. His throat swelled shut, and it was impossible to get even liquids down. He had to be fed intravenously for ten days.

Byrd, living with the scientists in the administration building, had not known about the group of tipplers, who had managed to keep their nocturnal gatherings a secret. But after Chip's accident, the alcohol drum was removed to Byrd's quarters.

On days when the cold got extreme, ranging from minus fifty to minus sixty with no wind, I learned we could hear our own breath freeze. I took a black satin cloth and held it flat and open in front of me. When I exhaled, I actually heard the hissing sound of the moisture freezing, and I watched in utter fascination as it dropped onto the black cloth. In less than a minute, I had enough frozen breath to pick up with my fingers.

We got used to the cold. As the days shortened, the temperatures dropped, preparing us for later. By the time we were in the minus forty range, we didn't attempt any work but concentrated on keeping warm. We had to protect our hands, never allowing them to get too cold: In those temperatures it takes only seconds for the hands to freeze. The most efficient hand wear then was wool mittens, on top of which we put fur mitts. We tied our mitts around our necks by a string to prevent our losing them should we take them off for a few minutes to work more easily with our fingers. When we were running with the dogs, if we ever dropped a mitt, it was too bad. The dogs moved so fast that we had no chance to stop and pick the mitt up.

We kept the fur hoods of our parkas up so that the wind wouldn't blow directly into our faces. At times all our faces froze, and it was painful when they started to thaw. Extending the fur of our hoods several inches beyond our faces blocked most of the wind. When we had to walk directly into the wind, we covered one side of our faces with the fur of our hoods. Every minute or so we'd shift the covering and cover the exposed side.

The whole time on the ice we wore goggles outside to prevent snow blindness because of the continuous white. Sometimes, however, the bottom rim of the sunglasses froze to the face. In pulling off the glasses, we often snatched off tiny patches of frozen skin. Sixty-odd years later I still have a scar under my eyes from this exposure.

The most important thing about body protection was to keep our feet warm. If our hands froze, we could still travel. But if the cold got to our feet, we were finished. Survival in the Antarctic meant we had to keep our feet dry. Wet feet in those subzero temperatures guaranteed a freeze-up.

We wore three pairs of woolen socks. On the outside we wore windproof socks made of cotton. I had used them while working with Dr. Grenfell in Newfoundland. The outer socks collected the moisture, and by the end of the day we felt as if our feet were immersed in water. We naturally took the socks off at night and hung them outside. When traveling, I hung them anywhere I could on the sled. Every time we passed, we paused to wring them out, and crystals of moisture fell away. Within twelve hours of freezing and being wrung, they would be dry again and ready to wear.

———————◆———————

Radio, still in its infancy, had many problems. On some days we had excellent reception from the station in Schenectady, New York, but on other occasions, we would lose words and sometimes whole sections of a transmission. Such skips were caused by changes in the altitude and density of the Heaviside layer. Now known as the ionosphere, this belt of ionized particles in the atmosphere refracts short-wave signals. Its distance from the earth's surface varies with time of day, season of year, and disruptions like sunspots. Such variables determine how many times a radio signal may travel back and forth before it reaches its intended receiver. If the signal skips over the receiver, there is a loss of transmission.

75

Our radio engineer, Malcolm Hanson, needed to spend a week on the ice away from Little America to study the ionosphere. He had to go to a place where huge steel objects like the radio towers and planes would not hinder the signals he would be broadcasting and receiving for the entire week. His calculations suggested that he needed to travel away from Little America approximately ten miles.

Always the volunteer, I jumped at the opportunity to accompany him. It meant getting away from our camp (and from Walden) and another chance to be involved in a new phase of the exploration. We could take nothing with us made of metal. That included belt buckles, eating utensils, sleds, coins, and keys. Even the dog collars were replaced with rope.

On the appointed day I had a sled all packed, including an adequate supply of easy-to-prepare food. We selected nine dogs and brought them out of their tunnel, the first time they had been outside for twelve weeks. As soon as the dogs came into the fresh air, they went wild with excitement. They were filled with such frenzied energy that it took one man to handle each dog. We put them in harness just outside the tunnel entrance. While waiting to leave, I anchored the sled to the radio tower so that the dogs wouldn't run off with it. Mike Thorne, an expert skier and pathfinder, would lead us out of camp and point us into the frozen land beyond.

The chilling wind was blowing at thirty miles an hour, and the temperature registered minus forty. Hanson, ready to go, was delayed for nearly ten minutes with last-minute instructions from the station in Schenectady.

When Hanson came out, he signaled to me that he was finally ready. In the middle of the long night and despite the cold, a dozen men lined up with flashlights and lamps, pointing away from the camp and expressing their best wishes for our success.

Just then Dr. Coman, standing near the sled, said, "Wait a minute." He pointed to the dogs.

They were facing downwind. In their excitement at going out on the trail, they were jumping and their tails were up wagging and waving around, exposing their rectums. Because of the intense cold and wind,

Coman checked the dogs closely. He shook his head, saying, "Their rectums are hard."

He meant that the dogs were freezing. Thankful he had noticed, I asked for help in unhitching the nine dogs. We took them back inside and selected nine replacements for the trip. This time I made sure Hanson was absolutely ready before the animals came out of the tunnel. With Hanson sitting in the sled, I pulled the harness safety line for the dogs to start. Mike Thorne pushed off on his skis, a flashlight strapped to his helmet. The flashlight made it easy to follow him in the almost moonless night.

Because of the heavy load they pulled, the dogs quieted down after two hundred yards. Pulling sleds equipped with wooden runners on cold, granular snow was like dragging weights over beach sand.

At the end of a mile, Mike turned on his skis and waved good-bye. I looked around and saw five other skiers coming up behind us. Assured we were all right, they turned to go back to Little America with Mike.

I deeply appreciated their gesture; they wanted to express their enthusiasm about the radio experiment. I believe their coming also showed the spirit of togetherness we shared in everything we were doing.

Once we reached a distance of ten miles from Little America, we stopped. Hanson helped me erect our tent. Next we carried his radio equipment inside, and Hanson set up everything for his real work to begin. While he did that, I staked out the dogs and fed them chunks of seal meat. I felt sorry for the dogs as I watched them gnawing away in that frigid temperature. It took them a long time to chew the frozen meat and get it soft enough to swallow.

While they ate, I took a wooden shovel and dug a hole two feet deep and four feet wide for each dog. It was imperative that I get them out of the wind. As soon as I finished, each dog dropped into his hole and curled up. Those holes would serve as their home for the next six days and nights.

After taking care of the dogs, I started preparing a meal for the two of us. About that time I heard a soft, mournful wail from one of the dogs. I went outside, and by torchlight I saw Ginger's pitiful eyes, telling me that she was really suffering from the cold. The poor dog was actually shivering. I unloosed her, brought her into the tent, and let her lie down inside my sleeping bag.

Ginger was so thankful that she lay still in the bag, making no sound. When it was time for me to go to sleep, Ginger hadn't warmed up yet. I got into the bag beside her, and the two of us spent the night together. As it turned out, Ginger spent the week in luxurious warmth — compared with the other eight dogs. On the trip back to Little America, she showed real spirit and pulled as hard as any of the dogs for the entire trip. Ginger's enthusiasm convinced me that giving her warmth for the first time in twelve weeks had paid off.

Hanson soon had his equipment operational. He wanted continuous reception between us and Schenectady to study the effects of the Heaviside layer, or ionosphere, so someone had to watch the dials constantly. Hanson and I worked out a schedule so that when he slept, I stayed awake. During his sleep, my only responsibility was to keep my eyes on the dials of his equipment. If anything changed — and they changed frequently — I had to awaken him immediately.

"Hanson! The dials!" That's the most I ever had to say.

As if a gun had gone off, Hanson would jump from his sleep and twist partway out of his sleeping bag so that he could reach the dials. He'd make some kind of adjustment and crawl back inside his sleeping bag. Within seconds he was sleeping again.

When we returned to Little America and Hanson appraised his work for the week, he said, "The mission was a complete success."

That work by Hanson greatly added to the volume of research done by experts who, using more sophisticated equipment, finally eliminated skip distances as a problem.

Even though my role was small, I felt that I had played a part in the advancement of radio technology.

Toward the end of the long winter night, our mess hall "head" filled almost to the top. We readily ascertained that it could not accommodate much more, and because of the snow cover, making a new one was not an option. So a poker game was convened to determine the unlucky losers who would have to clean it.

On a Saturday, the traditional sports day in America, we sat down after lunch at the mess hall table for our big-stakes game. Dr. Coman was unanimously chosen to be the dealer and keep the game honest. The game progressed through the afternoon. The lucky winners stood around, watching the consistent losers and their draws. Coman had to call for order more than once, when partisans made revealing comments about the cards being held. As winners left the table to join the on-lookers, the number of losers shrank.

In the middle of the game, we noticed that Gummy, our cook, was still playing. Someone suggested that our esteemed provider should not be exposed to chips and pieces from the monumental stalagmite. Cheers erupted, and by universal consent, a grateful Gummy was removed from the game.

As the cards were dealt, onlookers crowded closer. Tension mounted, and players became more and more protective of their hands as the winners called thinly veiled hints to the players left in the game. Suddenly I realized that only seven of us losers were left. I became very serious. I didn't laugh. I didn't do anything except look for three aces.

They never came, and when the last players put their cards on the table, I had the worst hand of all. Thus it fell to me to chip and shovel while a fellow loser hauled up the bucket and emptied it outside, on the barrier.

As I dug deeper, I called for a ladder. It would be my way out, protection against a prankster who might not pull me up. Finally, I had excavated seven feet of the eight-foot pile. My job was done.

More than anyone else, I appreciated my next visit to the head.

———————◆———————

During the long night on the ice, caring for the dogs was sometimes quite a chore. The dogs, having no work to do and being well fed, grew fat and beautifully covered with long, thick fur. They had energy to spare, and crowded around as we fed them, nearly knocking us over.

Because of the cramped space in the tunnel and the poor light thrown by our kerosene lanterns, we had a hard time keeping track of all the animals. Consequently, we didn't always know when the bitches were pregnant—sometimes not until the pups were ten days old. As soon as the pups' eyes were open, they could crawl in and out of the crates and would greet us at the doorway when we brought food.

We never kept track of the number of pups born, but we had quite a few of them, and most of them lived. We started giving them such political names as Roosevelt and Hoover. We named one pup Al Smith, after a rising Democrat who later ran against Herbert Hoover for the presidency of the United States. Al Smith became Gould's pet dog. Gould fussed over him, and gave him privileges that none of the other sled dogs had. Gould even brought Al Smith into the mess hall and allowed him into his own sleeping quarters!

We drivers detested that dog. For one thing, we prized animals for their ability to work, but Al Smith never won our admiration. He was lame, always sickly, and one of the ugliest animals I have ever seen. We should have disposed of him shortly after he was born, but because Gould favored him, we didn't.

To make it worse, Gould was convinced that Al Smith would be a great lead dog. We kept working with him, hoping he would get better and become strong like the others, but he never did.

Now, I admired Larry Gould more than anyone I have ever known. Although he was a renowned geologist and the second in command, he had such a common touch about him that at first no one could guess his education and background. Gould was unquestionably the most popular man on the expedition.

But his incurable optimism about Al Smith was incomprehensible. So one day we decided to get even with Gould for his preferential treatment of that ugly dog and have a little fun at the same time. We had exhausted the names of politicians and had moved on to explorers. There were pups with such names as Byrd, Scott, Mawson, and Shackleton.

We renamed Al Smith "Laurence Gould" and on his crate we hung a sign showing his new name. When Gould saw the sign, he said nothing, and turned around and left. His lack of response took a little of the fun out of our joke. The next day we read the following message on the mess hall bulletin board:

EFFECTIVE TODAY, NO DOGS WILL BE NAMED AFTER LIVING EXPLORERS.

Laurence Gould

The Commander

$\mathbf{A}$s our leader, Byrd had to live separately from us in a partitioned room off the library. I would expect that of anyone in his position. Yet he was always friendly and communicative. He called all of us by our first names. (Of course, none of us ever called him Richard or Dick. We all said Commander or sir when addressing him.) He participated in the jokes and pranks that went on all the time. We played a few on him, and he took them well. He even played a few on us, all harmless and in good taste.

Like a skipper on a ship, he had his own cabin and his own books. Because of contractual agreements to publish an account of the expedition, Byrd spent a lot of hours each day writing in his journal. He carefully recorded everything from temperatures to menus to daily activities and all happenings in the camp. (All of us had signed a statement declaring that we would wait at least one year after our return before publishing anything; I waited sixty.)

Byrd also had his own dog at Little America, a fox terrier named Igloo. I didn't pay much attention to Igloo, and neither did any of the other men, because Igloo paid no attention to us. He was keen on one man, his master. Many times Igloo would sit motionless as his master stayed quiet, staring reflectively at the dog. When the commander moved, so did Igloo.

We had only one mess hall and everyone ate there, including Byrd. One day he was sitting next to me. He chatted with all of us at the table, just as he did at any other mealtime. I was finishing my third cup of coffee, and everyone else had left the table except Byrd.

Byrd turned to me. "Norm, I'm going for a walk in about twenty minutes. Would you like to walk with me?"

"I'd be happy to," I said. He was the leader and I saw it as an informal command, even though he hadn't put it that way.

"You don't have anything to do," Byrd asked, "that you can't leave?"

"Nothing pressing."

"Good. Twenty minutes, then? At my house?"

He left, and as I finished drinking my coffee, I thought about his invitation. We all knew that the commander went out for a walk every day unless the weather was too cold or a storm was blowing. He'd walk briskly for forty-five minutes, always making certain he was never out of sight of the radio towers. As long as he could see them, Byrd could get back to camp. He once said that he did a lot of his best thinking during his walks along the barrier edge.

At first I felt pleased that he wanted me to go for a walk with him. Yet embarrassed, too. I assumed that if the others saw me walking with Byrd, they'd think I was playing up to him. But what did I have to gain? Byrd had brought me along on the expedition—the biggest favor he could have done for me. He had already asked me to head up the dogs for the geological expedition. What more could I want?

When we left for our walk out on the barrier reef, three men stood outside talking. I wanted to hide my head or walk behind him, anything to make them think I was not with the commander. But it was obvious that we were walking together.

We both wore fur parkas. The temperature, right at zero, made walking comfortable, and no wind was blowing. After a few minutes we pulled off our parkas because we had heavy wool clothes on underneath.

When I went with Byrd on his walk, I had no way of knowing that within two months he would invite me three more times. After the second walk, I realized that the pattern of conversation was the same. Our words started with the general and the trivial. Part of the conversation went like this:

"Well, Norman, how do you like it here in Little America?"

"It is the most wonderful experience of my life! I love it here." I meant every word, too.

"Everything going well in camp?"

At first I thought he might have heard about Walden and wanted to talk about it. I said cautiously, "It's still such a great adventure."

My answer seemed to please him, and he said so. "How are the dogs?" He followed up with other questions, such as, "I wonder how your family is doing with your being so far away?" "They are all happy, I hope?" "You are staying in touch with your family, aren't you, Norman?"

Then he said, "I hear nothing but good reports about your work on the expedition."

I thanked him for telling me. Naturally the compliment gave me a good feeling because I worked hard.

Within minutes, however, Byrd's tone changed and so did the content. Although I listened carefully to every word, I couldn't figure out what he was trying to tell me. It was one of those odd times when you know a man has something he wants you to understand but he speaks in such a way that you have to pick it up by inference. He did not normally speak that way. The vagueness impressed upon me the importance of grasping what he meant.

Byrd brought the term *my loyal legion* into the conversation. On our first walk, after he used the term, he followed it up with a seemingly casual question. "Norman, what does *loyalty* mean to you?"

Without giving it much thought, I said, "It's being faithful to your beliefs."

"What exactly does that mean?" he asked.

"Well," I said, having no idea where the conversation was going and even less idea what he was pushing for, "faithfulness means having a principle to stand for. You hold to that by the way you behave."

"Can you give me an example?"

I thought quickly and finally came up with one. "I don't drink, sir. That's a principle with me. I don't think it's good for our bodies, and you know I believe in taking care of our health — "

"Has your loyalty to this principle ever been tested?" he asked. "Have you ever had to face the matter of being loyal to that belief?"

"Oh, yes," I answered, ready for that one.

I told him about being invited to join the Spee Club at Harvard. I wanted very much to join but hesitated because I knew they always got the neophytes drunk during the initiation. When talking to the representative who invited me, I told him, "I can't do your initiation rites." He talked it over at length with club members, and they finally allowed me to join without taking a drink.

"And so," I told Byrd, "I was informed that I'm the only one in their history admitted without having a drink."

"Yes, yes, Norman," he said. "That is precisely what I mean about being loyal to principles and ideals."

During our conversation, I was concentrating on being loyal to what I believed. It did not occur to me that he was actually talking about loyalty to *people*.

I may have disappointed him that day because I spoke mostly in generalities. I didn't emphasize that I would be loyal to my commander. Being so young, I was intimidated by his rank, his age, and his role as leader. He was a retired commander in the U.S. Navy, and people everywhere looked up to him. The eyes of America — and the whole world — were on this expedition. I was still having a hard time believing I was part of it. I had no inflated ideas of my role. I considered myself nothing more than a cog in the big wheel.

Further, I was immature and inexperienced enough that I didn't fully grasp the purpose of our walks and talks until years after we returned to America.

But reflecting on the event, I think Byrd was afraid he would need to call on his men later to back up his claims of what had happened in Antarctica. It seemed important for him to know that if his critics tried to deny his achievements or disregard the data he had collected, we would stand loyally with him and tell the truth.

In retrospect, I also realize that Byrd put his questions so that they almost demanded my acquiescence. His words left me with the distinct impression that if I did not agree to support him unreservedly and thereby become a member of his loyal legion, I would not be one of the boys. And I wanted always to be one of the boys.

When Byrd took his daily walk, I soon noticed, he always had somebody with him. When I discovered that, I felt better, knowing that he had not singled me out. The other men had the same problem of embarrassment when Byrd invited them to walk with him. Consequently, no one ever said a word to tease the others. And no one refused to go when asked.

Byrd never walked with the same man two days in a row, and he walked with everyone except Larry Gould, with whom he met daily anyway. He never did call on me or any of the others for support. Only later would I realize how strongly he must have felt about being able to do so. Yet Byrd had nothing to hide. The expedition wasn't falsifying data. He reported only true information.

Years later, Bernt Balchen told me something that made me believe I had finally figured out Byrd's worry. After Byrd had made his famous flight over the North Pole in 1926, one critic questioned whether Byrd's plane had actually flown over the Pole. If such questions ever arose about the Antarctic expedition, Byrd wanted to be certain that he could count on our loyalty.

While still on the ice Byrd wrote a major article that took up most of the April 1930 issue of *National Geographic,* and the following year he published his book, *Little America.* Later that same year, 1931, Larry Gould published *Cold,* which substantiated everything Byrd said in print. So far as I am aware, no one ever questioned any of the information about Antarctica.

In my opinion, based on working with him in the 1929–1930 expedition as well as our close association in the 1934 expedition and my contact with him during the rest of his life, the charge about his 1926 flight was nonsense. Byrd was far too careful with the facts. He was no god, and he had his faults, but I never questioned his integrity—then, later, or now.

———————◆———————

During our walks on the ice Byrd himself told me a little-known story of how he almost didn't make his historic flight on May 9, 1926, in the three-engine Fokker, *Josephine Ford.*

On April 29, 1926, Byrd and his shipmates arrived at Kings Bay, Spitsbergen, to find the Amundsen-Ellsworth-Nobile expedition already there and assembling their Italian dirigible *Norge.* They planned to cross over the North Pole and proceed to Nome, Alaska. Italian mechanics were already at Nome, waiting to disassemble the *Norge* and return it to the Italian navy.

As for Byrd, his plane had broken three skis on test hops, and there wasn't any more hardwood to be found. Everything seemed hopeless until a Norwegian came over from the Amundsen camp to look around. His name was Bernt Balchen. When he saw the broken ski and the delay it had caused, he said, "I fix."

He used a closet door from Byrd's boat, shaping and fitting it into a replacement ski. Floyd Bennett made a test flight and the ski held. Before long Byrd and Bennett were off to the Pole.

Amundsen and Ellsworth were among the first to welcome Byrd back from his flight. Byrd considered them exceptionally good sports, for he had won the undeclared race to the top of the world with the help of Balchen — a member of Amundsen's own team.

In gratitude for his assistance, Byrd later brought Balchen to America. Balchen flew over the Atlantic with Byrd. And, of course, he joined our expedition to the South Pole as the chief pilot.

———————◆———————

One day Balchen told me of an incident that took place during the 1927 flight across the Atlantic — one of those stories Byrd didn't reveal to the public. He flew with three men, Bernt Balchen, George Noville, and Bert Acosta. Acosta, known as the best pilot for the feel of the stick, took the overloaded plane off the ground. He flew the first few hours, after which Noville relieved him.

In those days the planes had to fly fairly low. Acosta and Noville became nervous because they saw nothing but the ocean's whitecaps. The subzero temperatures, the dangers of icing up, the never-ending view of icebergs and ocean frightened them.

"We can't see anything but the ocean," one of them groaned. "We need to turn back."

"Let's have a drink," the other said. "I think it will settle our nerves."

"Good idea," the first one agreed.

The two men took a drink, but Byrd and Balchen refused. A second drink followed. They continued until both got drunk. Several times they begged Byrd and Balchen to turn around and go back to the United States.

"We can't make it!" they cried. "We'll die in this frozen ocean."

Byrd adamantly refused to turn back. Finally, tired of their drinking and raging fear, Byrd said, in a calm voice, "Balchen, take over the controls."

Back in the fuselage, Acosta and Noville continued drinking and complaining. At last Byrd left the cockpit and picked up a wrench. He struck first one, then the other, in the head, knocking them unconscious. They lay on the floor of that plane for the rest of the trip.

When they crossed the shoreline of France, Balchen spotted a lighthouse near Ver Sur Mer but could not see much else. They located Le Bourget field at Paris, but because of a heavy undercast and poor visibility, they could not land. They circled and circled Paris, and people on the ground heard the roaring engines. Radio spread the news all over the world: "Byrd is over Paris but cannot land."

In the plane, Byrd and Balchen, aware of their diminishing fuel supply, gave up trying to land at Le Bourget. They would have to find another place.

"The lighthouse," Balchen said. "Our only chance."

Byrd agreed, and they headed back to the lighthouse. Balchen landed in the shallow water about thirty yards offshore. Surprisingly, the plane did not turn over. Byrd and Balchen waded in to the beach.

"Two of my men hit their heads when we landed," Byrd reported to the people who welcomed them ashore, "and they're injured." To save their honor, Byrd fabricated a story that Noville and Acosta had been in the fuselage without being strapped in and had struck their heads when the plane landed.

Fortunately, no one ever questioned why two men should have matching welts.

Our winter was soon coming to an end. I didn't mind the long night, but I eagerly awaited spring. When spring arrived, the geological party would go out on the ice for three months. And most exciting to me, Goodale, Crockett, and I would go along with Larry Gould. Gould put me in charge of the dogs — a dubious honor, as I was to learn later.

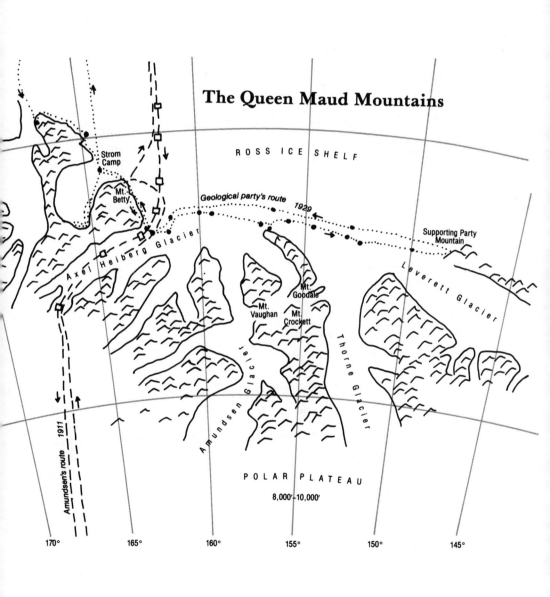

The Queen Maud Mountains

R O S S   I C E   S H E L F

Strom
Camp

Mt.
Betty

Geological party's route

1929

Supporting Party
Mountain

Axel Heiberg Glacier

Leverett Glacier

Mt.
Goodale

Mt.
Vaughan

Mt.
Crockett

Amundsen Glacier

Thorne Glacier

Amundsen's route 1911

P O L A R   P L A T E A U

8,000'–10,000'

170°   165°   160°   155°   150°   145°

Overland

On August 20, 1929, the sun returned. Several of us climbed the radio towers for a preview of its rays. From our vantage point, the icy land magnified the rays of the flaming disk by refraction. Not until August 24 did the sun rise high enough for all of us to appreciate it from ground level.

How can I explain the joyousness of the first few days of sunlight? We felt like prisoners who had received commutation of our sentences. A brightness appeared on our faces. We walked faster and moved with an energy we had long forgotten.

The dogs, released a few at a time from their weeks of darkness, raced around Little America, yelping and barking. Although they scrapped and occasionally attacked each other, they could do nothing to deflate us. My lead dog, Dinny, who had nobly proven himself over the months we had been unloading the two ships, raced around in an uncontrolled frenzy. He acted more like a stallion let loose on the prairie than a dog. I gave up trying to calm him down.

Commander Byrd, caught up in the moment with the rest of us, ordered all forty-two of us to assemble outside the mess building. In a short, solemn ceremony, we unfurled the American flag. Martin Ronne, representing the Norwegians, then raised his country's colors. Canadian Frank Davies followed with the Union Jack. In his brief remarks, Byrd honored our predecessors from those two nations. (All three flags stayed up and flew until we abandoned Little America.) In the background, a Victrola played the bugle call to arms. At Byrd's signal, we uncovered our heads despite the chilling winds. Then the commander said a prayer, thanking God for bringing us through the long winter night.

———————◆———————

Daily we noted the sun's lengthening stay and closely followed the weather conditions. Our records showed that we had received 93.8 inches of snow between January 1 and September 8, although half of it had blown away in the high winds.

Each day the sun rose a little higher, remained visible a little longer, and slowly advanced to the east. It began as a yellowish blur, distorted by refraction, peeping over the horizon and awakening the slumbering drabness of the Ross Ice Barrier. We enjoyed only slight relief from the cold during the rest of August through September. Temperatures rested between forty below zero on August 31 to minus sixty-six two nights later.

We had quite a laugh when we heard that New York City's temperature on September 4 was ninety-four degrees above zero. I quickly calculated that in Antarctica our thermometers registered a difference of one hundred fifty-seven degrees.

Eager for our real work to begin, we forged ahead on plans for the expedition. Byrd had broken the mission down into three parts. First the supporting party would set out. Next the geological party would depart, and finally Byrd himself would attempt a flight over the Pole.

The situation with Walden took care of itself when the sun reappeared. Activities speeded up. Walden no longer had time to brood. We worked outside more, and I became absorbed with final preparations for Larry Gould's geological expedition. And of course, I soon left Little America with the overland explorers.

Two weeks before our departure date, Byrd put me in charge of laying bases for our final trip south. I made up a small party of men, and with our sleds loaded with food, we headed two hundred miles due south toward the South Pole. We laid caches every fifty miles.

The laying of caches was standard for exploration in Antarctica. By putting out food for the geological party, we could lighten the loads we would carry when we left Little America for the real trip.

A cairn of ice blocks piled six feet high marked each food cache. We set up bamboo poles with orange flags every twenty-five yards to the east and west for one mile. Daylight would soon be almost twenty-four hours a day, and no matter how bad the visibility, we would be able to pick up the orange flags, the easiest color to identify against the snow. By mid-December we would have continuous, unrelieved daylight.

The orange flags were almost an unnecessary precaution, we discovered when we set out again. Since we traveled due south, with the sun to our backs, each snow cairn gave off a white glare. Like a silvery tower, it acted as a mirror against the white sky and the white of the snow. We could see as many as three shining caches ahead, reassuring us that we were on the correct trail. When we looked toward the sun, we were unable to see a single orange flag after we had gone a mile or two.

I never had the fear of getting lost in trying to get back to Little America as we laid the caches on our outward journey. Although the trail was covered by new snow, our dogs sensed the direction and kept on it very well. We were careful, however, and checked our route constantly with a large compass on the leading sled. It floated on gimbals, so the minute we stopped the sled it would settle down and give us a magnetic reading. The deviation in the Antarctic was tremendous because the needle was pulling toward the south magnetic pole, and we had to take this deviation into consideration at all times.

———————◆———————

After a whole winter being isolated at Little America and working every day on the preparations for the trail, it was a tremendous relief when we left on the geological party. If all went well, we would cross and recross the Amundsen trail. That was exciting enough, but I also kept thinking that after the polar flight, we were actually going to travel on land that no person had ever set foot on before: for me the most important aspect of the entire expedition. *And I was part of it.*

Everyone in camp came out to say good-bye to us. George Tennant, our cook, always thinking of our stomachs, shoved a small box into my hands.

"We're already packed tight," I told him.

"You won't have to worry about the weight of this," he said.

"What is it?"

"Lunch." He grinned at me.

He had packed sandwiches made with bread fresh from his ovens. Because he used dry meat, the sandwiches didn't put a lot of ice into our mouths. Had he made sandwiches with a soft filling, we would have eaten as much ice as food.

Except for the first two hundred miles, which the advance party had traveled a week before, the trail ahead was unknown to us. We were heading toward the South Pole. I was so excited, I could hardly wait to get on the trail.

The geological trip had a double purpose. First, we had to be as near to the South Pole as possible on the day Byrd made his flight. We were to function as his rescue party should he have to make a forced landing. Byrd wanted us to have enough men and dogs, food, and equipment to be equal to the task that Amundsen had performed in 1911 when he went to the Pole and back. We could not plan on any help from the air. That was a stipulation Byrd gave us when I started my logistical planning. He insisted that we operate as an entity.

Second, after Byrd's successful polar flight, we would turn our attention to the geological work under Larry Gould.

On October 29, 1929, a line of dog sleds started across the first slope of the barrier. The rolling plain of snow, leading into a vast ice wilderness, was tinted in soft rose. The flaming sun in the western horizon seemed to urge us on. Mike Thorne glided ahead on skis, watching for crevasses we might encounter. Guided by a compass, he set a straight and accurate southern course.

Gould, Goodale, Crockett, Thorne, Jack O'Brien, and I made up the entire geological party. We left a month before Byrd's flight on November 27, with food enough to go all the way to the South Pole and back without air assistance. We joked, "The only thing we won't carry on our sleds is the air we breathe and the water we get from melting snow"—but we did have to carry the gasoline to melt the snow.

———————◆———————

Our first week on the trail, Larry Gould developed a blister on his left heel from skiing with his socks twisted. Without saying anything, he tried to continue. On the sixth day, just as we started on the trail, Gould casually said, "I've got a little blister on my heel."

"Want me to take a look at it?" I asked.

He shook his head. "It'll take care of itself in a day or two."

I didn't argue. But several times during the day I noticed a limp or, when he was close, a wince of pain. When we stopped that evening, I asked, "How's the heel blister?"

"About the same." His tone told me that he did not want to discuss it and that he regretted even mentioning it.

In the cold tent, after supper, I insisted. "Larry, let me see the blister."

"It's not that important—"

"You're limping and I can tell the blister hurts. And it might get worse." Gould was a tough man, and I had to beg him to let me look at his foot. He finally agreed.

The blister, the size of a half-dollar, had broken open and was weeping. Although in intense pain, Gould kept insisting it would get better. The spot couldn't possibly get better as long as he permitted it to keep rubbing. After applying a liberal amount of antiseptic salve around the blister, I formed a doughnut-shaped pad from the felt innersole of one of my boots. After ensuring that the hole was big enough for air to get to the blister, I made the pad double thick, about one-quarter inch. Putting his foot into his boot the next day was difficult because of the thick spot around his heel, but Larry did get it on eventually. More than a week elapsed before he could walk and ski without great discomfort.

I relate this account for three reasons. First, a simple thing like an unattended blister could have jeopardized the whole exploration trip. Second, Gould was the man who did the scientific work; we went to assist him. Without Gould, there would have been no scientific party. Third, Gould never complained about the intense pain. Not once did he hint or suggest that he ride on the sled to ease it — and doing so would have been acceptable to all of us until his blister healed. He was a tough man who demanded the most from himself. That is part of the reason I admired him so much. By his own example Larry Gould inspired the rest of us to give our best.

As our self-appointed cook, Gould prepared our breakfast of oatmeal and coffee, tea, or chocolate. Because the beverages came in powder form, we could have our choice without making things complicated for the cook. He devised a clever plan for our breakfast. Each night Gould boiled water, added oatmeal, and poured the mixture into a large thermos. By morning we had a warm breakfast already cooked. On Sundays the chef added raisins to the cereal.

We all had wooden bowls and wooden spoons so that when Gould filled them with hot hoosh or cereal, the food wouldn't cool off as rapidly as it would have in lightweight aluminum.

We established the daily routine of getting up in the morning and going out to our dogs, harnessing them, and tying them back into the gang line. They would immediately lie down and wait until we gave the command to go forward. Everything else done, we took down the tents and packed them on our sleds.

———————◆———————

Mike Thorne, the best skier on the expedition, led us on our route south. Traveling with a pack on his back, he carried about twenty-five pounds of clothing or food to lighten the load for the dogs.

Thorne stayed anywhere from fifty feet to half a mile ahead, giving me guidance. That meant I did not have to yell "Gee!" (to the right) or "Haw!" (to the left) when breaking trail. As our pathfinder, Thorne constantly sought the best route for us to travel. For hours at a time, he scrutinized the landscape, searching for the only real danger we faced: the crevasses, or great cracks in the ice, into which we could tumble. Falling in would have meant certain death.

To understand how dangerous these crevasses were, and why they were so difficult to avoid, one needs to know how they come about. The Ross Ice Barrier is a mass of ice floating on the ocean. It starts at the Queen Maud Mountains, where glaciers flow down to the sea and join contiguous glaciers, forming a huge shelf of ice extending four hundred miles to the north.

The slow northward movement of the Ross Ice Barrier is undisturbed except where its base encounters landforms that rise from the ocean floor. At such points the top of the glacier continues its forward motion, pushed by the tremendous pressure of the river of ice behind it, while the bottom of the glacier is obstructed. The pressure causes great cracks in the ice. Eventually, the bottom works its way over the obstructions, causing more cracks and disturbances at the surface.

These crevassed areas are frightening because not all the cracks are visible. Blowing snow can form bridges over crevasses, concealing them from view. In the white landscape it was difficult to identify the bridges, which could break under the weight of a sled. The crevasse would swallow the loaded sled, and the free fall would pull the whole team of dogs along with it. They would all disappear.

Years earlier, in fact, when Sir Douglas Mawson was traversing the ice, he paused on one occasion and turned around, expecting to see a team of dogs directly behind, guided by Mertz. But Mawson saw only the vast white stretches of this frozen continent. He waited a few minutes, thinking Mertz might be lagging and hidden behind a rise. When Mertz still did not appear, Mawson retraced his own steps. Right in the trail over which he and his own dogs had gone was a gaping hole on the surface of the Antarctic barrier. Mawson's team had probably weakened the bridge. When Mertz came along, following Mawson's tracks, the bridge cracked and broke, and Mertz, his dogs, and his sled fell into the crevasse.

Sir Douglas listened but heard nothing. He shouted and finally detected a few whimpers from a dog, but soon he heard only silence. There was nothing Mawson could do but offer his prayers for his departed companion.

No ropes, no ladders, no means whatsoever can rescue people from a deep crevasse. The typical crack has a wide opening at the top and narrows as it goes downward. When falling bodies—whether men or dogs—hit the bottom of the crack, the impact of the fall wedges them deep into the ice, just as if a giant hammer has pounded them in. Even if they are still conscious, they cannot move. They quickly die of exposure.

Knowing that if we ever fell through a crevasse bridge, we would perish, Mike Thorne remained vigilant. He looked for cracks. He looked for anomalies in the snow cover. He looked for any indications that we were in a dangerous area. And he tested suspicious-looking terrain.

When he suspected a bridged-over crevasse, he would violently strike the snow with his ski pole. If the crust covered a crevasse, one of two things happened. The bridge might break, in which case we did not attempt to go across, and Thorne had to select a safe trail around. Or, he heard a hollow sound that confirmed the existence of a crevasse below. He would then appraise the width and direction of the crevasse and the thickness and strength of the bridge, and decide whether we could cross. Naturally, he had to be cautious and think of the difference between his weight and that of the oncoming teams.

If he thought the crevasse was narrow and the bridge would support us, he put up flags that instructed us exactly where to go. We crossed at a right angle to the direction of the crevasse. We did well until one day a sled slipped sideways, broke through the bridge, and ended up straddling the crevasse. Had the crevasse been larger, we would have lost the sled and maybe even the team and its driver.

A crevasse only two feet wide could have been disastrous if we drivers had been on foot. Thorne might have skied over such a crevasse at right angles and never known it was there, since his skis would have spanned the crack. But a man on foot could fall right through. For that reason, during the entire trip, we skied alongside our teams, rather than dogtrotting, as we had during the freighting operation.

Crevasses wider than eight feet or so were less dangerous because we could see them — snow and ice bridges did not usually span such large gulfs. Still, we were careful. I recall the first big crevasse we encountered. Thorne zigzagged around, seeking out solid snow as best he could. He set up flags every few feet to indicate which path we should follow to get safely around the crack.

We drivers constantly searched for crevasses ourselves. It was always possible that Thorne might unknowingly cross a thin bridge, weakening it for those who followed. Yet Thorne never made a mistake, and his trails were always safe — *almost* always, that is.

One time, after we had started exploring the Queen Maud Mountains, we climbed on Mount Nansen to an altitude of six thousand feet. Gould decided we would spend the night there. The next morning, as we were starting down the same glacier we had ascended the previous afternoon, Mike Thorne abruptly stopped. Still about a hundred yards in front of me, he raised both arms and held his ski poles between his hands, over his head. This gesture signaled, "Stop at all costs. Do not proceed. Danger immediately ahead."

Instantly I put all my weight on the gee pole and tried to stop the dogs. We were going downhill, on ice, and the sudden braking caused the sled to skid and slide toward Thorne. Those behind me had enough warning to stop, but my sled was now careening toward Mike at a dangerous speed. I called to the dogs, "Haw!" They swung to the left. That helped, but I knew we would still not stop in time. In those few seconds I realized that my only hope of survival lay in turning the sled over. I leaned on my gee pole and, using all my body weight and strength, managed to turn the sled onto its side, bringing everything to a halt with the lead dog less than two feet from Thorne.

Mike was standing on the edge of a crevasse four feet wide that had opened up during the night. We shook our heads in disbelief: We had climbed over the same spot sixteen hours earlier.

Panting and shaking a little, I untangled the dogs. Fortunately, I was all right, and none of the dogs were hurt. It might have been a far more frightening experience had I had time to think about it. Once we were safe, a crevasse no longer held the threat.

101

"I thought John Harvard was going to crash and burn!" said the stalwart skier. A Yale graduate, Mike Thorne kept a friendly rivalry going with the three musketeers from Harvard.

"I didn't want to run into that Yale bulldog so I thought I'd pull up," I said. "Why did you stop? I could have jumped four feet."

"Just wanted to see if you could stop! I didn't think you'd break your sled, though."

Sure enough, a runner had split in two, and I could not use the sled for forward motion. So I turned the sled around and put the broken runner to the rear. Because we had double-enders, I still had two good runners in the front.

As soon as we were back on the trail, we proceeded along the eastward extension of the Queen Maud Mountains. I put the incident with the crevasse behind me. It was the only way to stay mentally healthy. Dwelling on what had happened (or what might have happened) would only prevent my giving full attention to what lay ahead. I could think about the danger later. Right then I wanted to concentrate only on the adventure of the trip.

► *Norman D. Vaughan, 1928.*

▼ *Preparations for the expedition's dog drivers began in Wonalancet, New Hampshire, under the tutelage of Arthur T. Walden, who had hauled freight in the Alaska gold rush. Young Norman Vaughan's lead dog, Dinny, got along well with Walden's Chinook, but relations between the two men were less amicable.*

▲ *Vaughan's Harvard classmates Eddie Goodale (center) and Freddie Crockett (right) soon joined the expedition. The three musketeers, as they were known, trained dogs for Byrd.*

▼ *Taking an idea from the igloos Walden had seen in Alaska, the young men built dome tents, which could withstand the strong winds that sweep across Antarctica.*

Experimental Tent 58. "Karluk," 6 mos. old, Chinook Kennels, Wonalancet, N. H.

▲ *Scotty Allen (standing, right) visited Wonalancet to swap old Yukon tales with Walden and, as Alaska's winningest racer, share his expertise in driving dogs. On Allen's advice Vaughan left behind Storm, his one-eyed Newfoundland: a slight irregularity in the dog's gait indicated that he would tire on long trips.*
PARAMOUNT NEWS PHOTO.

► *Vaughan modeled his caribou mukluks while Cocoa, one of the ninety-seven expedition dogs, lazed in the winter sun at the foot of the White Mountains.*

▼ *The sled dogs' harnesses had adjustable, padded leather collars. Note the wooden spreader that prevented the webbing from chafing the dog's rear legs.*

▲ *A team of Chinooks, led by their namesake sire, pulled a test load of two thousand pounds over the trails at Wonalancet. Walden wielded the gee pole to keep the sled upright around a turn.* PARAMOUNT NEWS PHOTO.

▼ *On a Norfolk, Virginia, pier Goodale, Vaughan, and Crockett waited to board the* **Sir James Clark Ross**, *a Norwegian whaling factory, for the voyage to the Southern Hemisphere.*

► *The tail of a blue whale dwarfed a crew member of the whaling factory. In 1928 whales were not known to be endangered, and whale meat was a staple for the expedition.*

▼ *Final supplies were loaded onto the* City of New York *(left) and the* Eleanor Bolling *at Port Chalmers, New Zealand.*

◀ *To unload the* City *at the Bay of Whales, expedition members — both men and dogs — worked around the clock. Large chunks of frozen whale meat hang from the rigging.*

▼ *Putting a Ford on skis with an endless track over the wheels sounded like a good idea — it's the same principle as a modern snowmachine — but the ungainly assemblage dug itself into a grave every time it was hitched to a load. Dog teams were the better idea.*

▼ *Expedition headquarters, known as Little America, were erected quickly from prefabricated components at a site nine miles from open water, on the Ross Ice Barrier. Soon snow would bury everything except the three radio towers; supplies and gear not marked with poles were covered and lost.*

1262-131

▲ *A quarter of a mile from Little America, twelve whales surfaced in an open lead. After four days the ice shifted and the whales disappeared.*
▼ *In his capacity as expedition ornithologist, Paul Siple conducted necropsies on emperor and Adelie penguins. Siple later became an antarctic explorer in his own right.*

▲ *The animosity between Arthur Walden and Norman Vaughan had escalated, and the younger man now had reason to believe that his life was in danger. Fearful that Walden might attack him in his bunk at night, Vaughan would leave the relative warmth of a Little America bunkhouse to sleep in a tent outside.*

▲ *Watching emperor penguins toboggan on their bellies was a pastime until the sun set for the antarctic winter. Penguin meat, along with whale and seal flesh, supplied some of the needs of the camp; at least one of these rich meats was on the table every day.*

◄ *Crockett holds one of the camp's favorite pets, Belle, after she was bitten in a fight. As a member of the geological survey party, Belle displayed extraordinary stamina and courage.*

► *Dinny, Vaughan's most reliable lead dog, was also injured in a canine scuffle. His master performed the necessary surgery.*

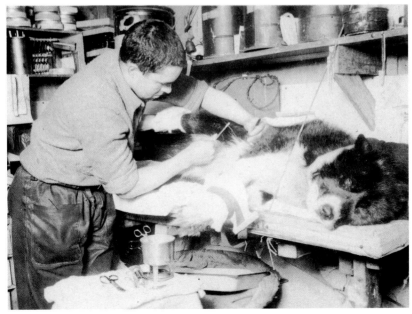

Every night there was enough hot water for two baths. Any man who wanted a bath more frequently than once a month could roll in the snow. No one tried that a second time, however.

Cook George Tennant baked bread every week and varied his menus with stews, chowders, roasts, and puddings. Word of his iceberg creation, chocolate-covered ice cream on a stick, reached General Foods; by the time expedition members returned home, a commercial version was in production and on the market.

▲ *Amusements during the long ant-arctic winter included table games and gambling. A stake limit prevented cardsharps from wiping out the novices. On Saturday nights everyone gathered around the radio to hear a special broadcast from Schenectady.*

► *The hoarfrost on Laurence McKin-ley Gould's surveying equipment made it difficult for him to make his observations. He needed regular read-ings from his theodolite to determine whether the Ross Ice Barrier, on which Little America had been built, was still attached to the continent or imperceptibly adrift.*

► *Gould was second-in-command and leader of the geological survey party, which included the three musketeers. Besides surveying a portion of the con-tinent, the explorers would provide emergency backup for Byrd's flight.*

◄ *When spring came, Vaughan selected the forty-six strongest dogs to pull the sleds for the geological party; the men would ski alongside. Moody emerged from a tunnel and sniffed fresh air for the first time in three months. This dog and his brothers Watch and Spy were the power trio in Vaughan's team.*

► *Martin Ronne, sailmaker for Roald Amundsen's 1910 race to the South Pole, was one of the senior members of Byrd's expedition. So that the overland explorers could be spotted from the air in an emergency, he sewed orange markers into their tents.*

▼ *The fourteen-foot freight sleds were heavily laden with a three months' supply of food and fuel for six men; as the loads became lighter and the dog food ran out, the weak animals would have to be killed. The bicycle wheel at the back functioned as the party's odometer.*

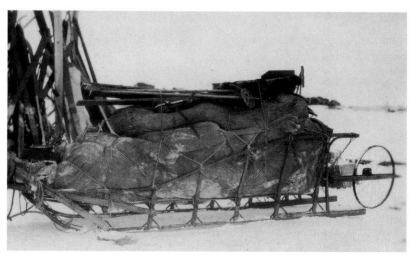

▲ *Pressure ridges made overland travel a constant struggle, and crevasses concealed by thin bridges of drifted snow were ever-present dangers for both dogs and men.*

► *While Vaughan (right) cranked the generator, Crockett made the regular call to Little America. Camp chores included digging a shallow nest for each dog in the hard-frozen snow; a shovel stands ready.*

▲ *Close to Amundsen's cairn the geological party built one of their own, where they left an American flag, a sled with a shattered runner, and a short written summary of their mission. Left to right: Vaughan, O'Brien, Crockett, and Thorne.*

▼ *Byrd's Ford trimotor, named the* **Floyd Bennett** *after the pilot who had flown with him to the North Pole, had to be warmed by blow torches. The motor oil, meanwhile, was being thawed on the camp range. Note the three-bladed and two-bladed props.*

Holding a flag and a stone from Floyd Bennett's grave, Richard Evelyn Byrd paused at the door to his study in camp. During his historic flight the next day, he let both tributes fall to earth over the South Pole.

Weary and grubby but elated, the overland explorers arrived safely home to Little America. Eddie Goodale and Jack O'Brien are standing, with Mike Thorne, Freddie Crockett, Larry Gould, and Norman Vaughan on the sled. Among the surviving dogs was Vaughan's leader, Dinny, who sat patiently behind.

Belle

The story of Belle sums up so much about my feelings toward sled dogs. It also explains a lot about this wonderful breed and about why we dog men become so attached to our animals.

During the winter Belle escaped from her crate and got in a bloody battle with another bitch. I found Belle lying in the seal house, covered with blood and unable to move. Because she was chewed up so badly, she was allowed into the semiheated machine shop to recuperate. While she was there, she became something of a camp pet. She was gray and had flop ears and brown eyes. She wasn't especially good-looking, but she loved to be petted. Her constantly wagging tail and bright eyes earned her everyone's affection.

Belle was in my team on the geological party. We knew she was pregnant when we started, and that marked her as the first to be killed when the time came to diminish dog power on the trail. We took her along because she was such a tiger at work; no animal ever gave more of itself. I watched her carefully. Had she shown any signs of suffering, I would have killed her immediately. We had to sacrifice our dogs to help feed the others, and I accepted that. But I did not, and would not, allow our animals to suffer.

One night a whimpering from outside the tent awakened me. I got up and went out to see what was wrong.

Belle had given birth to one pup and was giving birth to a second one. I took the first pup, killed it, and buried it a few feet away. Using my shovel, I dug down one spade depth into the ice, making the hole just big enough for the pup. Belle watched me intently as I did this.

In our situation we had no choice. Pups could not possibly survive because we were on the move. We couldn't carry them on our sleds, and given our limited rations, their mother couldn't feed them without depriving the other dogs. We had all agreed that killing them was the most humane solution.

When Belle's second pup came, I did the same thing, burying it in almost the same place. After burying both pups, I checked Belle, but it didn't look as if she would have any more. I returned to my tent and went to sleep. In the morning I found two more pups lying next to her. Not allowing myself time to think about the unhappy task, I took the babies from her and buried them with the other two.

After breakfast I checked on Belle again. She was down on all fours when I came out of the tent. As soon as she spotted me she stood up with her tail wagging, intently watching my every movement. I looked her over carefully. To my amazement, after having delivered four puppies she looked peppy and ready for a day's work.

I put her in harness with the others, and we started our day's trek. Belle immediately used all the strength she had and pulled the sled about five yards to the left side. She stopped where I had buried her four puppies.

I was on skis on the other side of the sled from Belle. Before I could do anything to get her back on the trail, Belle rooted in the snow and dug them up one at a time. Then she swallowed them whole, just as fast as she could.

Her behavior shocked me so much I could do nothing but gape at her. I had never seen or heard of anything like it before. I wasn't revolted, but I felt a terrible sadness that Belle had to eat the pups I had taken away from her. She simply wouldn't go off and leave those four pieces of herself. I pulled myself together, still saddened.

By then the other teams had pulled out. Usually I skied in front, right behind Mike Thorne. But that morning I waved the others on and yelled, "Go ahead! I'll come along as fast as I can." I wanted to be sure Belle could carry on before we left. She seemed fine, and I figured we could leave. By now we would have to hurry to catch up.

Belle stepped forward with the other dogs and started to pull. Suddenly she stopped, and her neckline became taut. The rest of the team started to drag her a little. I yelled, "Whoa!" Her hind end sloughed down onto the snow, her legs were out to the left side, and she would not move by herself. The other dogs dragged her a few feet before stopping. They didn't like being left behind by the other teams.

Belle was in the middle of the team. The other dogs had their ears up and were looking at her. Before I could get to her on my skis, she lifted her leg and produced a fifth pup.

I was absolutely stunned. I started to lean over and take that pup away when she stuck her head down and swallowed it. "Oh, God, no," I moaned, feeling terrible that she had been reduced to eating her own babies. Belle was doing the kindest and wisest thing possible, but I still felt as if I had failed her.

The other teams, moving farther and farther into the distance, were barely visible. I couldn't lose much more time or they would disappear completely. We had no time to stop, so I backed up my skis to the gee pole and gave the signal to go forward. Belle, by then on her feet, pulled with the other dogs, behaving as normally as ever.

Twice more that morning, Belle gave birth as she pulled her load on the trail, making a total of seven pups. She went through the same motions, having the other dogs drag her a few feet and grabbing and swallowing each pup as quickly as it was born. Then she immediately moved back into position and pulled her weight.

As sad as I felt about the situation, I admired that dog for giving me every ounce of her strength and yet having the sense to know what she had to do with her newborns. She continued to pull as forcefully as the other dogs for the rest of the day.

As a way to show Belle my sympathy, I offered her a whole cake of food when we stopped at noon. She refused it. Again at night I held out a two-pound cake, but she wouldn't eat anything. I understood and did not try to force her to eat more.

That night common sense said to put Belle down, but I just didn't have the heart to do it. When we made camp, she lay down and went to sleep just as she had in the past. She had no signs of afterbirth or any kind of difficulties. Her teats had not given out any milk, although they were slightly swollen.

"Well?" Gould asked gruffly. "What about Belle? When are you going to take care of her?"

His gruffness didn't fool me. He didn't want to see the dog die any more than I did.

"Let's wait until morning. If she isn't all right then, I'll take care of things." He understood the meaning of my words.

I knew that if I didn't kill Belle in the morning, one day soon her suffering would force me into action. Her exposed teats would freeze, and then she would really suffer. But I loved Belle as much as any of the animals, and because she had shown so much spirit, I kept hoping I wouldn't have to dispose of her.

When morning came, Belle eyed me as I crawled out of the tent. She snapped herself to attention, letting me know she was ready to go. My team led off, and Belle pulled as hard as any dog I've ever had. I had to steel myself not to get upset over her. Such work must have taxed her strength, but that wonderful dog stayed right at her task. Not once did she slacken the line and force the other dogs to pull her. For the next two days, Belle kept pace with all the animals on my team. Yet I couldn't let her go on. During the day the temperature never registered warmer than minus forty. I could see her shivering, and she almost fell down when we stopped to rest. The exposure was getting to her, and she was beginning to suffer.

Gould said nothing; he only stared at me. In reply I nodded, indicating I was ready.

Being in charge of the dogs, I had also accepted the responsibility of killing them. It didn't come easily and was never accomplished indifferently. These were dogs I had trained and cared for. That they were necessarily expendable did not help me when the time came.

Of all the times I had to kill a dog, disposing of Belle was the worst. I wept.

Our three-month survey party started out with forty-six dogs. I shot twenty-five of them before we returned. We scheduled it so that when we had lightened enough of our load to leave off a sled, we did away with five dogs at a time.

We began the trek with two sleds for each of the five drivers. We pulled our two sleds in tandem, chained together. When we lightened the load from one sled, we dropped it and disposed of part of the team. When we disposed of the second five dogs, a whole team was gone, so we dropped the remaining sled.

The dead animals provided food for the surviving dogs. Killing the dogs for food sounds cruel. Today nobody would consider letting the working dogs eat their own. In this modern era, parties can use snow-mobiles or air support to supplement supplies. But in those days—sixty years ago—feeding the dogs to each other was the accepted way of travel for explorers. Otherwise, we could never have gone on such an extensive overland survey because we could not have carried enough provisions with us.

On the trail, far from seals, we carried only the dog food I had prepared in New Zealand. We couldn't carry seal meat from Little America because it was heavy with water and would have weighted us down.

In planning for the trip, I had figured that each dog's daily ration would be one two-pound meat cake. Because of the heavy pulling they did and the intensely cold temperatures, two pounds a day wasn't enough for them. We had to sacrifice the twenty-five dogs over the three-month period to provide sufficient food for the surviving twenty-one. When I had to kill dogs, I saved the tails for our lead dogs. They stripped the tail and ate the cartilage for the little gristle that was on it.

◆

The first thing we did when we decided to stop at the end of a day was set up our tents. Each tent housed three men. The three musketeers shared one, and the other three men slept in another. We had a third tent where Larry Gould cooked our hoosh.

The cooking tent had no floor, but it did have a kind of skirt that lay on the inside. We dug a circular ditch six inches wide for our feet. This left a round, daislike section for a table, and we set the Primus stove on it. Once we had our feet comfortable and we were relaxed in a sitting position, Larry Gould filled our bowls and passed them to us.

Bowel elimination was a significant problem on the trail. No man would willingly expose his bare flesh to those temperatures, so we figured out a practical method. After breakfast we packed away the food and equipment. One at a time, each man went back into the cook tent, followed by his favorite dog. The animal sat patiently and waited while the donor (as we started calling him) squatted in the trench and defecated. As soon as he finished, he gave his signal, and the dog eagerly ate the fecal matter. It provided a bonus in food for the day and was actually good for the animal. After everyone had his turn, we struck the tent and put it on the sled.

We always packed the tents and sleeping bags last so that they could be the first things off at night to give us immediate protection in case of emergency. In addition, we carefully divided each load as to kind so that if one of us dropped into a crevasse with a team, the survivors would still have tents, food, and essential equipment.

We hit the trail, proceeding toward the Queen Maud Mountains. Each day I felt a growing excitement because we were edging closer to virgin land.

Great Discoveries

We encountered the worst storm of the entire trip three weeks after we had left Little America. Heading south, we were crossing a badly crevassed area. In the middle of that dangerous section a heavy wind arose, and it appeared to be getting stronger. Gould halted our travel for the day, and we all joined in hastily setting up our tents. Pelting snow stung our bodies as we labored to anchor everything. By then we knew we could do nothing until the storm blew over. The blast of snow struck so furiously that we had no idea whether the snow came from the sky or whether the powerful wind raised it off the ground. It didn't really matter, though: The effects were the same.

Gould finally decided that a strong wind had picked up the snow and was blowing it along the surface at a furious speed. Two hundred feet above us the sun was probably shining.

As the storm increased, with winds so strong a man could not stand up, clouds covered the sun's powerful glare. As always when outside, we wore glasses to prevent snow blindness, yet we could see nothing but the whiteness of snow as it pummeled us. We took refuge in our tents, which were close so that during the occasional lulls of the blow we managed to yell back and forth. But no one ventured outside.

Because I remembered exactly where I had packed the dogs' food on the sled, I volunteered to go outside and feed all the teams. My sled was the nearest to the tent I shared with Goodale and Crockett. Thankful for my volunteering, they crawled into their bags and soon slept.

To be absolutely sure that I could get back to our tent, I tied a rope around my waist before crawling outside. I tied the other end around Crockett's arm. I stretched my hands out to feel in front of me and inched forward. Twice I tried to stand, but the wind was too overpowering. Though I am six feet and weighed nearly two hundred pounds, this wind was no respecter of weight: It exceeded an estimated velocity of seventy miles per hour.

After what seemed like an incredibly long time of crawling, my hand touched the sled. Encouraged, I fought to unlash one section. Purely by feel, I counted out six cakes of dog food for my team. Since the animals were still harnessed to the sled, I expected to find them lying down in front of it. As I peered through the surging barrage of snow I could not see a single dog. Momentary panic arose in me. *Did they get loose and run off?*

Still going purely by feel, I crawled on. Then my knee went down and landed on one of the wheelers, the dogs closest to the sled. He moved, but I knew I had not hurt him. In his physical recoil, however, he uncovered enough so that I could see him under all the snow that had blown over him and provided a blanket of protection.

I passed a meat cake to the wheeler, but he refused to eat under those conditions. I found the other wheeler, and she refused as well. Moving on to the next pair of dogs on the gangline, I held the food up to their mouths, but they refused to munch or even take it. Obviously, none of the dogs would eat that night, so I stopped offering food.

The rest of the animals were lying under their covering of snow, so I decided to return to the tent. The wind seemed to increase its intensity. Hugging the ground, I scooted forward on hands and knees, following the rope back. Had I tried to stand up, the wind would have blown me downwind, probably knocking me over.

I reached the tent and crept inside. We hated bringing in snow, but I had no choice. I had to get out of my snow-filled parka. In taking off my parka in the crowded tent, I scattered snow over the sleeping bags. I brushed it off Crockett and Goodale as much as possible and piled the extra snow in a mound near the tent opening, where we kept our shoes and outside clothing. The entire effort had exhausted me, but my reward came when I crawled inside my own sleeping bag and fell asleep immediately.

We were somewhat concerned that the drifting snow might completely cover our tents and prevent our getting out. Fortunately, that didn't happen. But on the leeward side, which was near the door, the snow piled up so much that it pressed the cloth into the tent and diminished our air space. This problem caused us considerable anxiety. If the storm worsened, we would have to shovel out the tents while fighting the pelting snow. It would have been impossible in that storm to take each tent down and erect it again.

The storm continued for thirty-six hours. We stayed in our sleeping bags the whole time. When we decided the storm was over, we excitedly crawled out. Within minutes Larry Gould had put his culinary skills to work and was calling us for a meal. It consisted of oatmeal, peanut butter and biscuits, and plenty of hot tea. We were delighted to have anything to eat; I was so hungry I thought it was a great treat.

It took us six hours to dig out the three tents and the sleds and get the dogs ready for the trail. I felt we should have been able to move faster, and yet we worked as rapidly as we could. With every step we took, snow covered us up to our knees, and that doesn't make for fast walking—or easy shoveling. The dogs actually had to crawl up out of their deep holes.

By the time we started on the trail again, the weather had cleared. The sun smiled down as if no storm had ever passed our way. The wind had blown the soft snow away, so the traveling was smooth. The temperature warmed, as it often does after a storm. For the first seven days on the trip from Little America, the low temperature each day had been at least minus forty. Then it became noticeably warmer because the sun was higher, and our average low was only ten below.

◆

Our trip progressed satisfactorily along a route due south. When we were nearer the South Pole than we were to Little America, Byrd made his flight to the Pole and back, a total distance of sixteen hundred miles. On the same day as his flight, we first glimpsed the Queen Maud Mountains, over which Byrd's plane had to climb. Those mountains were our objective. Many days would elapse before we reached them, however: We averaged only twenty miles a day with our overloaded sleds.

On his way to the Pole, Byrd flew along our tracks at a low altitude. When he was directly over us, a small parachute fell from the plane. We raced to pick it up and brought it back to Gould. We discovered notes from our friends at the camp and extra food from George Tennant. Among the items Tennant had included were a prune pie and a heavily spiced angel food cake. The prune pie was so succulent we ate it from our bowls with spoons. For two days we ate richly and heartily.

More important to us than the food were the cables the parachute drop contained from our families back in the States. As we learned later, two weeks prior to his flight Byrd again showed a sensitivity to his men. He sent word to each of our six families, asking them to wire back a special message, which he would handle himself. The unexpected gifts warmed our spirits and made it one of our best days on the trail.

We decided that our expedition had another achievement to add to its growing record: Byrd had delivered the world's most southerly cablegrams.

I still have the parachute those messages came down on, along with the cable from my parents. They told me the news from home, all of it good, and wished us success on our historic journey. Hearing from them and being informed of their support and of their acute awareness of our geological mission touched me emotionally. Unconsciously my fingers fumbled through my layers of clothes to touch Father's watch. In a mystical way, I felt as if he stood beside me on the trail.

After Byrd's successful flight, we turned our attention exclusively to the geological survey. We headed east into land never before seen or walked upon by human beings. At night (by our watches), while our dogs rested, we climbed the nearest peak. From there Gould meticulously photographed all mountaintops in view. With his theodolite, he shot bearings, laying out a mile baseline some seventy-five miles away. Through this line he computed the positions of all the succeeding mountains: some navigational feat using only a theodolite and compass. The resulting map, keyed to a carefully measured one-mile baseline, matched within a few feet the photographic maps made much later by the National Science Foundation.

———————◆———————

Each day brought us closer to the Queen Maud Mountains. On December 8, 1929, we started on what we assumed was an easy climb. Before long, the deceptiveness of the land became obvious. The exposed rocks that were our goal for the day turned out to be farther away than we had thought. The absence of trees or any familiar object by which we normally estimate such things, along with the extraordinary clearness of the Antarctic air when the sun is high and has dispelled mists and clouds, made it impossible to gauge distances accurately. To make our travel worse, on every side we encountered innumerable bottomless crevasses.

Instead of camping, Gould directed the party to continue up to a huge gap in the high mountain wall that was the Axel Heiberg glacier. After reaching an altitude of forty-eight hundred feet, we stopped, amazed to finally encounter an area not filled with impassable crevasses. The covering of ice and snow was so heavy that we saw few patches of bare rock. Yet it was those bare rocks Gould wanted to reach.

Leaving the dogs behind, we roped ourselves together — our only provision for safety — and started up on our skis. Despite steep and slippery slopes, we kept going. It was a long, arduous climb, and we encountered several hidden crevasses. Each of us knew that with just one serious slip the whole party would be swallowed up without a trace.

Gould later told me that the longer we climbed, the more depressed he became. But after several thousand feet up the Axel Heiberg glacier, he let out a yell. "There! There!"

He discovered exactly what he had come for. He raced forward, forcing us to move at his pace. Then he paused, bent down, and picked up a rock the size of a hand. *It was yellow sandstone.*

"Finding this stone," he said to the rest of us, "has made every hardship worthwhile."

The piece of sandstone was part of the large mass of flat-lying rocks that topped the big mountains like Nansen. The presence of sandstone proved that the mountains were actually gigantic blocks of the earth's crust that had been pushed from sea level into the air as high as fifteen thousand feet. Between these massive blocks were deep depressions that formed rifts (or ditches) and were occupied by mammoth glaciers like Axel Heiberg, the one we were on.

Some two hundred miles to the west, a geologist with Scott's expedition had discovered the same geological formation with the same structure that Gould now found. Our discovery confirmed that the Queen Maud Mountains were a continuation of the mountains on the western borders of the Ross Sea. Gould now knew we were on the largest mountain fault system in the world.

Gould didn't find any fossils in the sandstone, although geologists have since located them in other parts of the Antarctic. On the lava rocks, however, we found a lot of lichen, a symbiotic association of fungi and algae. It was the farthest south anyone had ever seen these plants—another plus for our scientific efforts.

That night Gould sent the following radiogram to Byrd:

> No symphony I have ever heard, no work of art before which I have stood in awe ever gave me quite the thrill that I had today when I reached out after that strenuous climb and picked up a piece of rock to find it sandstone. It was just the rock I had come all the way to the Antarctic to find.

The climb up the glacier had been over such a rough route that we decided to go down more smoothly and safely by traveling in the middle of the glacier. This route offered fewer crevasses, and the whole surface seemed smoother than along the eastern side, where we had come up.

Thorne, taking the lead as usual, stopped suddenly. Unsure why, he said, "I've got a sense that something is wrong."

None of us could see anything ahead that should cause him concern. But we had learned to trust Thorne's judgment. Still roped together, we retraced our steps down a more gentle slope. Two hours later, while we were sliding down the new trail, Thorne stopped, turned, and pointed back to where he had insisted on stopping and retracing our steps. We could now see that we had been within five feet of the edge of an immense cliff that would have been a drop of at least a hundred feet— and probable death.

Before we moved farther eastward, we wanted to locate Mount Betty, where Amundsen had built a cairn on his journey home from the South Pole. At Mount Betty he and his party had left the only written record in Antarctica of their long journey. To find his cairn and definitely identify Mount Betty at the same time would tie our work with his.

On December 10, when we came down the glacier, Gould decided we should turn right and go over to a peak that he thought might be Mount Betty. At noon we arrived at the foot of the mountain and stopped for lunch. This was the first place in our travels on the geological party that we had been able to drive our dogs right to the rocks—the first the dogs born in Little America had ever seen.

We had a little fun watching the animals experience the strange objects. At first they stared at them but shied away. Finally Al Smith approached gingerly and sniffed for a familiar odor. Another dog, Dinty, licked a rock. Not being able to eat it, he lost interest. As if Dinty had been their leader, the other dogs thereafter ignored the rocks.

After lunch we tethered the dogs and climbed the rocky outcrop. Amundsen's records stated that Mount Betty was twelve hundred feet, yet our barometer gave us an altitude of twenty-six hundred. We saw no other mountain or rock mass that could possibly be the one he had described. After a careful search we found nothing that resembled a cairn. Disappointed, we went back down to our camp. I wondered if we would ever find Amundsen's cairn.

◆

We stood at the foot of the Queen Maud Mountains, and I knew we had enough food and equipment to go over the range to the South Pole. Byrd had made it clear before we left that the geological party would not be going to the Pole unless we went there as a rescue party for his plane.

We never reached the Pole, but we came within two hundred seventy-three miles of it. As our two predecessors had proved and subsequent overland voyagers confirmed, the route from our closest point to the South Pole itself was a relatively easy one. I'm sure we could have made it to the Pole and back, had that been our purpose.

Instead we went eastward into unknown land. We traveled along the Ross Ice Barrier at the base of the mountains, avoiding heavily crevassed areas and continuing the same routine every night after we made camp: We tethered the dogs, ate, and then climbed the nearest mountain. When we made our nightly climbs, at least one person stayed in camp with the dogs, the sleds, and the tents.

We knew the importance of keeping alert on the climbing ventures. Going up and down every night demanded total mental and physical concentration. Perhaps that's why whenever any of us returned from the climb, we immediately wanted food. The one who stayed in camp prepared hoosh for the climbers before going to bed. He left the food in the pot, ready for heating up.

When the climbers were close enough on their return to see the tents, they whistled. The noise alerted the dogs, who were not used to any outside commotion. They didn't move, just lay on the ground and raised their voices in a cacophonous howl. Their noise would arouse the sleeper, who would raise his arms from his sleeping bag and start the Primus stove.

By the time the climbers reached camp, the man at the base had hot water and hot hoosh ready and had gone back to sleep. Upon settling down, the others ate lustily and soon got into their sleeping bags for the short remaining night.

Usually the same four men went up. Jack O'Brien, whose specialty was surveying, ought to have gone up every night, but Gould ended up doing the surveying most of the time while O'Brien stayed below. He had lost interest in the surveying, and he didn't like climbing. The rest of us, on the other hand, seemed to become ever more enthusiastic as we progressed into the unknown.

———————◆———————

We kept up radio communication with Little America on alternate days. On December 19, Crockett made contact with the camp, and he yelled out to us the good news: By a special act of Congress, Commander Richard Evelyn Byrd had been appointed a rear admiral.

As much as anything that had happened, that piece of news convinced us that America was aware of our presence on the ice. Our leaders had honored Byrd, and we felt they had honored the expedition as well.

Five hundred miles north of us, Byrd had skirted the coast of the continent that marked the eastern boundary of British exploration. The new lands he discovered to the east he claimed for the United States; in honor of his wife, he named them Marie Byrd Land.

No one had ever set foot on this American-declared portion of Antarctica. Gould believed that questions and counterclaims might arise because the United States was basing its ownership solely on the flight over a new land. No nation had ever made such a declaration. In trying to set this precedent, the United States might end up in an international dispute. We wanted to back up Byrd's stake by reaching the eastern boundary of his claim. That would make us the first people to actually walk on land within the American section of Antarctica.

Once we reached our destination, Gould named the mountain Supporting Party Mountain to honor those involved in the preliminary work that eventually brought our geological party to that place. On December 21, 1929, we had come to the farthest point east from Little America of any walking human.

We decided our historic journey would not be complete without a ceremony of some kind. We piled up stones six feet high to make a cairn. Then we attached a small American flag to a bamboo ski pole and planted it. Our voices rang with joyous excitement. Suddenly, as if a hand had signaled for silence, we stopped speaking. All six of us stared at the flag as the wind rippled through it.

In unison, as if directed by a military command, we took off our hats and pushed our parka hoods back. We snapped to attention.

A wave of emotion spread over me, as I suspect it did with the others. So much had happened in the past sixteen months, taking me from college to this triumphant moment in Antarctica. My fingers automatically pressed against my layered clothes until I felt Father's watch. The sense of his presence was as strong as it had been the day we landed on the ice. I wished he could have been with me in this proud moment.

After several seconds of silence, Gould stepped forward. In a husky voice he said, "Hats on!" It was a moment of deep satisfaction and achievement on the journey.

Taking a page from his notebook, Gould wrote down the names of all of us in the geological party. In a bold hand he continued:

> We are beyond or east of the 150th meridian, and therefore in the name of Commander Richard Evelyn Byrd claim this land as part of Marie Byrd Land, a dependency or possession of the United States. We are not only the first Americans but the first individuals of any nationality to set foot on American soil in the Antarctic.

Gould inserted the message inside a weather-protected can. We placed the can inside the cairn on top of Supporting Party Mountain.

Upon our return to America, we learned that the State Department accepted Gould's statement but did not choose to recognize the claimed land as part of the United States. The United States set the principle of working cooperatively toward what eventually became the Antarctic Treaty, by which sixteen nations jointly govern the entire continent.

The treaty states that the nations will review the Antarctic treaty in 1991 to determine whether the continent will continue to be governed by the same or similar management. Emerging Third World countries now object to a pact in which sixteen nations arbitrarily control this vast, untapped land.

An alternative to a continuance of the Antarctic Treaty is to open up the Antarctic continent for individual nations to stake claims.

In my opinion, a treaty arrangement is the wiser solution. Otherwise the policies for fishing and mining and preservation of birds and animals will be different in each claimed area, which can only lead to trouble and possible bloodshed. We have too much warfare all over the globe. I would like to keep Antarctica the one peaceful area where science can prevail and organized mining and fishing can be carried on with benefits for all humanity.

The Final Try

People frequently ask me how we washed clothes during our eighty-seven days away from Little America. We worked that out quite simply.

Each of us carried one extra set of underclothes. After two weeks on the trail, I said to Larry Gould, "Well, we've had a lovely dinner. The wind is calm. I think it's time for me to change my underwear tonight." Though the temperature was not warm, it would be simple to make a fast change.

Gould stared at me and scowled before he bellowed, "Hell, no! You will not change! Norman, you're an explorer! You'll go on wearing what you are now wearing."

He was in charge, and I said, "That's fine with me." I could stay in the same underwear as long as he could.

At the end of the third week, Gould said to all of us one night, "Gentlemen, we've had a lovely dinner. We have a nice night. Tonight is the right time for all of us to change our underclothes."

We made a grand party of the underwear-changing event, celebrating it as one of the high points of our first three weeks away from Little

America. We put on our new set of underclothing and packed away our dirty underthings. What a grand feeling—as if I had just enjoyed a Saturday night bath. That change of clothes gave us such an uplift, we made five extra miles the next day.

Everybody was happy, and we kept talking about how nice our bodies felt. We wore the second set exactly twice as long as the first. Then, at Gould's command, we put the first set back on, and they seemed clean by comparison. In that way, we had "clean" clothes for the whole trip.

———————◆———————

Gould made the decision to head back toward Little America on December 23, 1929. We had found the mountains getting progressively lower and the ice and snow covering thicker.

I know that giving the order to head back was tough for him. Not so much interested in reaching the Pole, Gould wanted to push on farther to the east. He was convinced that by continuing another hundred miles, the geological party would find answers to a number of geological questions our exploration had already raised.

Yet as he well knew, we had limited supplies, especially the dogs' food. We had worked those animals terribly hard and didn't want to subject them to additional difficulty. Several were already limping; all were showing the strain. None of them could now work at the capacity they had started with two months earlier. Our food allowance of two pounds of meat cake per dog was inadequate for the physical demands placed on these faithful animals. They really needed closer to four pounds a day.

We traveled at night so that the sun, which shone continuously, was at our backs, as it had been on our outward journey. It was always well above the horizon as it completed its circle every twenty-four hours. The reflection of sunlight also turned the snow beacons marking our food caches into pinnacles of bright light. In miragelike conditions, they appeared to be five degrees above the horizon.

Recrossing the ice field was as hazardous as the original trek, and we had to stay alert as we followed the bamboo-flagged course of our outward journey. Such concentration demanded a great deal from us, especially since all of us were already exhausted and our dogs had slowed considerably.

A constant hazard to our sleds was the sastrugi—ridges of snow that had developed parallel to the wind direction through the wearing away of the surrounding snow. Sastrugi are usually only a few inches high but are so tightly packed that they have the hardness of ice. The rough sastrugi shook our sled lashings loose and gave the sleds a real beating. Although they had held up remarkably well, the sleds were showing the effects of constant abuse. We had already abandoned seven of them before we started the return.

———————◆———————

On Christmas Day, 1929, while still at the mountains, we planned to sleep at Strom Camp, where we had set up our tents when heading eastward. Gould stopped along the way occasionally to make astronomical observations, and we continued on westward up the slopes to reach our designated spot. We encountered a heavy blanket of soft snow along the foot of the mountains, increasing the hardship for us and the dogs in making our way through it.

Gould finally said, "Stop!"

We wisely quit eight miles short of Strom Camp because of our exhaustion. To continue would have been cruel to our dogs. Having traveled through the night, it was early on Christmas morning when we halted.

For me, that Christmas was the most beautiful day on the trail. So often when the sun is bright, only the far-off snow takes on color. But as if nature had presented a special Christmas gift, the snow around us, normally dull and chalky white, glistened with a myriad of changing colors. Perhaps it was the loose snow covering everything that enabled the sun to turn the land into glorious Technicolor. Whatever the reason, I had never seen such overpowering natural beauty in my life.

We made camp at the foot of the eastern side of the mountain, which we had originally thought might be Mount Betty. After all we had seen on our eastward journey, Gould had concluded that no other mountain could fit Amundsen's designation. Yet we had tried and failed to find the cairn Amundsen had left there. Not locating that landmark had been the single big disappointment of our now two-month journey.

At seven o'clock on Christmas evening, which had become our morning, Gould said, "We're going to give it one more try."

He spoke only those words but with a set jaw and a determined edge to his voice. All of us knew what he meant. The party would make one final attempt to locate the Amundsen cairn.

Since we had previously searched the top of the mountain, we knew the cairn could not be there. Gould pointed to a shoulder of rock that projected northward about a thousand feet below the real top of the mountain. We had not examined that section before because it didn't seem conceivable that Amundsen would have referred to such a small ridge as Mount Betty.

Gould was so skeptical that the ridge might be our long-sought cairn, he agreed with me not to drive the dogs the extra distance to investigate. He and Thorne decided to ski over to the ridge. If they thought they had found the cairn, they would signal back, using two trail flags.

The distance, about three fourths of a mile, was largely a downhill slide, so it did not take more than minutes for them to reach it. Gould told us later that what had appeared as a single rock in the field glasses at camp took on a different view as he got closer. He could plainly see it was actually a series of rocks that had been built up, one stone on top of another. *Such a pile could only have been put together by human hands, and those hands could only have belonged to the Amundsen party.*

Gould waved the two orange flags wildly. We jumped into action, hardly believing the signal. Our stupor vanished; new energy infused us all. The dogs, previously tired and listless, responded to our excitement. We raced toward the ridge. Finally, panting from exertion, we reached the two men. They were sitting on the ground, chatting and looking around casually, as though they had come for a picnic.

"What took you so long?" Thorne asked. "Oh, I forgot—that's typical of Harvard boys, isn't it?" This time the three musketeers were too excited about seeing the cairn to rise to Thorne's bait. I staked the dogs instead.

Without a command, we moved forward. Together the six of us approached the cairn as if we were encountering a holy shrine. Upon reaching the cairn — and it was indeed Amundsen's — none of us spoke a word. Reverently we pulled a few rocks off its side. We did not want to disturb the shape or structure of this great monument. Reaching inside, Gould pulled out the things Amundsen had left eighteen years earlier. We found a five-gallon can of petrol and a waterproof package with twenty small boxes of safety matches. The cache contained one other item, a tin can sealed by a tight lid.

Gould paused as he stared at this treasure, knowing before prying off the lid that he held in his hands what we had most sought — an account of Amundsen's history-making journey.

His hands trembled as he displayed the tin can so that all of us could see. Using a pocket knife, he pried off the lid while we watched in fascinated silence. He pulled out two small sheets of paper torn from a notebook. One page gave the names and addresses of Amundsen's men.

We did not have to be able to read Norwegian to get the sense of the second piece of paper. Dated 6–7 January 1912, Amundsen's letter stated he was writing to tell the world that he had reached the South Pole. He listed the names of his companions and said he hoped to get back to his own camp successfully. If the crevasses opened up and swallowed them, he wanted this to be a note to the king and citizens of Norway as well as to the rest of the world that he had reached the South Pole on December 18, 1911.

Gould copied the entire note, letter by letter. He knew enough Norwegian to make it legible. He then wrote a brief description of our geological party and recorded that we had taken the note and the matches from Amundsen's cairn. Finished, Gould placed the notes inside the can and kept Amundsen's original.

The six of us, more than any other people alive, understood the significance of Amundsen's achievement. We had walked and skied over the same ice and snow. Our own experiences enabled us to grasp what it had cost him and his men to make the journey and to leave the simple message.

Gould gave each of us permission to take a small piece of rock with us but added, unnecessarily, that we must in no way disturb the cairn. He also gave each of us two boxes of the matches. We wanted to leave the cairn looking like it had when Amundsen and his men built it.

As we walked away Larry Gould paused, turned back, and saluted the cairn. His simple gesture conveyed the admiration for the Amundsen party that all of us felt.

Years afterward the Norwegian College of Academics honored Dr. Gould with a prestigious award. He went to Norway for the presentation by King Haakon VII. At the end of the ceremony, Gould said, "Your Majesty, I have a gift for you." Gould presented the king with Amundsen's original note. The king was overjoyed.

That note is now displayed in an Oslo museum.

———————◆———————

A few days before we discovered Mount Betty, I had to dispose of Al Smith, Gould's pet dog. Afterward, in an attempt to dispel Gould's gloom over his loss, I jokingly said, "I saved the tender joints for us."

"I'll starve before I eat dog!" O'Brien said.

"When you get hungry enough, you won't mind," Gould said. "We'll eat Al Smith later." He never said when. Gould's spirits eventually lifted, and he didn't mention his feelings of loss. Yet I knew him well enough to recognize that the stoic silence covered a deep grief for his canine companion.

The day before we discovered Amundsen's cairn, we stopped as usual. We set up the tents, and Gould started cooking the hoosh.

Jack O'Brien said to Gould, "Since the Strom camp is only ten miles away and the land between here and there is good, I'd like to ski over there."

"You might want to rest up," Gould said.

"Naw, I'd like to go. Besides," he added, "I've run out of smokes." For some reason I never understood, O'Brien had left his cigarettes at Strom

Camp. He was the only one of us who smoked. Gould, appreciative of the fact that those who did smoke longed for cigarettes when they ran out, said, "You can go, but don't do anything else." He added, "Be sure to stay right on course. If the weather holds, you should make it in good time. And come right back."

By the time O'Brien returned, we had all eaten and climbed into our sleeping bags. I had had to eliminate five dogs, so I was still awake.

Gould, too, like a mother keeping vigil, was still awake when O'Brien returned. "Jack," he said, "we saved some hoosh for you. It's mighty good tonight. Probably the best-tasting we've had on the trail."

"I'm sure hungry," O'Brien said.

"Yes, it's mighty good," Gould replied. "Norman put some of Al Smith into the hoosh."

"Don't tell me things like that," Jack said, not sure whether Gould meant it. "It isn't funny."

"Oh, he did." Gould had the marvelous ability to control his intonation and face so that no one could tell when he was joking. "Norman promised you that he was saving the choice bits of Al Smith for later."

"Aw, I don't believe that—"

"It surprised me how delicious it tasted," Gould said, ignoring O'Brien.

Jack O'Brien said nothing more.

"Well, glad you're back safe. Have a good supper," Gould said, and added, "Good-night." Pretending to go to sleep, he covertly watched O'Brien take the cover off the hoosh, stare at the mixture, and spot what he thought was Al Smith. Actually it was a piece of dried beef we had been saving for a special meal. O'Brien jerked back, almost dropping the hoosh. He made a horrible sound and breathed deeply, as if to force himself not to vomit.

He pushed the hoosh aside and muttered something about "damn cannibals." That night O'Brien's dinner consisted of crackers, a bowl of tea, and one of his cigarettes.

The next morning, Gould invited O'Brien to eat the leftover hoosh.

"I don't want any of—of that," he said, refusing even to look at it.

"You're sure?" Gould asked.

127

O'Brien lit a cigarette.

"All right, then," Gould said, "but old Al Smith sure flavors this nicely." He divided the hoosh among the rest of us. We ate as if it were the finest meal we had ever tasted.

"Norman," Gould said after taking a few bites, "we need to do this again."

"Too bad we don't have any more dogs to add flavor," I said.

Goodale called to O'Brien, who was walking away in utter disgust, "You missed a treat last night. And it's even tastier this morning."

I'm not sure we ever told Jack O'Brien the truth.

————————◆————————

Of all the adventures we had with dogs, nothing matches the story of Dinty, who had been the leader of Mike Thorne's team during the unloading of the ships.

Our party had started from Little America with forty-six dogs. Now we were down to twenty-one, the number I had figured we would need for the return trip. Because he was such a hard-working dog, Dinty was not only included on the geological survey, but he also numbered among the survivors who would return to Little America with us. Unfortunately, on the way back Dinty developed a bad shoulder. The rigors of the trail gave none of the animals a chance to recover. I recognized that Dinty would not be one of the survivors and reluctantly marked him for disposal the next day. Perhaps Dinty sensed what was happening. He lay quietly through the night without a wimper, even though he had to be in pain, and he refused to eat any of the diminishing supply of dog food.

"Norman, not him. Not Dinty," Mike Thorne said when he learned what I was going to do.

"Just look at him!" I pointed to the dog. "He can't pull with a shoulder like that. And we can't haul him on a sled until he gets better."

"But you can't kill him!"

"Listen, Mike," I said, "I know you're attached to Dinty. But there's nothing either of us can do about it. He has to go."

We had set the policy about dogs, and I was ready to enforce it.

Mike, however, appealed to Gould. After a lengthy discussion, Gould decided I shouldn't kill Dinty.

"Do it this way," Gould said. "Set Dinty free. Let him follow along at his own pace."

"I agree," Thorne said. He would have agreed to anything that gave Dinty a chance to survive.

I shook my head. "I'll do it if that's how you rule, Larry, but I think it's cruel. That poor dog can hardly walk. Dinty can't possibly keep up. He'll lie down and starve to death."

"Dinty will make it," Thorne insisted. "You wait and see!"

I didn't argue with Gould's ruling. When we started on the trail the next morning, Dinty seemed confused because he was not harnessed with the rest of his team. We started off, and Dinty, limping along, followed behind us.

At what we called noontime, we made a half-hour break for hot tea, chocolate, and biscuits. Just as we were ready to pull out, Dinty showed up. He was hopping along on three legs.

Although I had mixed emotions about all of this, I was hoping the dog would make it to camp. Yet I didn't see how Dinty could continue the trip with that bad shoulder. We couldn't leave food for him if he lagged behind.

Once Gould called for us to stop for the night, we busily set up our tents. Every few minutes my eyes scanned the horizon, searching back over the trail for Dinty. He never appeared. I fed the animals and joined the others in eating our hoosh. Still no Dinty. When making my final check on the dogs before going to bed, I spotted Dinty hobbling into camp. A lump filled my throat; every step must have been torture for that brave dog.

Wagging his tail, Dinty kept hobbling and finally sat in front of me. "Dinty's here!" I yelled, knowing that the others, although not willing to admit the fact, were as anxious for his appearance as I was.

Mike rushed out of his tent and watched silently while I fed Dinty. After eating, the animal lay on the ground next to his former team. Once again, I never heard a whimper out of him, despite the pain he surely felt.

The next morning our party started off again. As my team pulled out I turned to see Dinty limping behind us. Emotions tugged at me, wanting this brave dog to make it while hating to know of his terrible suffering.

On the trail the constant vigilance we needed kept our minds from dwelling on Dinty. When we stopped at noon, we did not see him. That night all of us delayed going to sleep, waiting for the dog to limp into camp. None of us said we were waiting, but we all knew. I had just about given up when Mike Thorne spotted him. He put on his skis and raced out to pick him up and bring him into camp.

This situation went on for two more days, Dinty taking longer and longer to reach us. Finally, we were breaking camp after our night's sleep when Dinty hobbled into our midst. I couldn't stand looking at him and thinking of his pain. I was ready to tell Larry we were being cruel to that animal and demand permission to put him down.

Just then Thorne rushed over to Dinty and fed him. We were already a few minutes late in getting started, but for once no one said anything about the delay. I think all of us were concerned about Dinty and not sure what to do.

Mike was not entirely the tough, unemotional man that he claimed to be. He picked up Dinty, who must have weighed forty-five pounds, and carried him away from the sleds. Without a word to anyone, Mike took off his backpack and retied it so that it would hold Dinty. He hoisted the forty-five-pound dog on his back.

No one said anything for what seemed like an incredibly long time. Then Goodale said, "Mike, let me help." He took Mike's pack. Goodale's initiative spurred Crockett and me into action. Among the three remaining teams, we divided up the twenty-five pounds of supplies that Mike normally carried.

Mike Thorne skied the rest of the way — for eighteen days — with Dinty strapped to his back.

When we left Little America, Thorne took Dinty to the States with him. Three years later Mike was running a bush-country airline in Canada that brought in supplies for trappers, hunters, and construction people. Dinty was still his constant companion.

Journey's End

We left Strom Camp on December 30, 1929, heading north to Little America. The first day we took a different route, hoping to miss several large crevasses and still get back on our trail.

The second day all of us felt a little anxiety as our eyes peered ahead, searching for our first orange flag or snow beacon, which we had erected a month earlier on our trip out. All afternoon our eyes scanned the barren landscape, but we saw nothing. Late in the afternoon I heard Crockett yell, "There it is! I see it!"

He kept pointing dead ahead. "A snow beacon," he insisted. While no one argued, I couldn't see anything, and neither could the others.

Another five minutes passed before Gould cried out, "That's it! Crockett's right! Straight ahead."

As if the beacon had miraculously appeared on the horizon, all of us saw the wonderful blinking light. Instinctively we moved a little faster, eager to be back on our original path. We hit the trail within a half-mile of where Gould had projected.

When we approached the beacon, I was surprised at how the blocks of snow had diminished in one month because of wind erosion and ablation. Evidently warm winds sweeping down from the mountains had depleted the snow. The outer blocks around our supply cache had icicles several inches long hanging from them; the blocks themselves were pock-marked from the melting. Fortunately none of our supplies had been exposed to the sun, so they suffered no harm.

The farther northward we went, the more we appreciated how well we had marked the trail. When the sun was bright, the snow beacons reflected light with a kind of blinking that we could see from as far away as six miles. Without them we could never have seen the flags from that far away. Although we navigated by compass, the flags and snow beacons gave us ongoing reassurance that we were on the right trail.

On days when the skies were overcast, we couldn't see the beacons, and we relied on the flags. Since we encountered more cloudy days than clear, the flags were indispensable. Several times the party traveled in fog so dense that I could not see the team moving only feet behind me.

The six of us were feeling quite robust, but the dogs were showing the strain of travel. Because of them, Gould limited our progress to twenty-three miles a day. When we came upon a good sledding surface, we made our miles quota in six hours and then stopped. Several times all of us would have preferred to push on another ten or more miles, but we didn't.

I constantly watched the dogs. If necessary I would have insisted on shortening the daily mileage. Huskies work hard and will pull until they exhaust themselves and never complain. That made it even more important for me to monitor their condition.

We hated fog on the trail—and feared it. January 9, 1930, was our worst time with fog. On that day Gould ordered us to make camp, thinking conditions might be better the next morning. When we awakened, we discovered an even heavier fog. To avoid delay we pushed on, but the thick atmosphere forced us to creep along. Not until late that afternoon did it lessen. Shortly afterward, exhausted from the mental and physical strain, we stopped for the night.

While we were eating our meal, several sharp cracks interrupted us. They sounded like rifle shots. We looked at each other in amazement until Gould said calmly, without expressing any concern, "The ice."

The thick ice was cracking, forming new crevasses and widening others. Both the intensity and the frequency of this cacophony increased. Before long we felt caught in a bombardment of guns going off around us, interspersed with muffled cannons firing from a far distance.

One of the cracks occurred right under our tent. The jarring made me spill my coffee. Gould reassured us that we had nothing to worry about. The possibility of a crevasse opening beneath us that would be wide enough to swallow us was remote. He explained what we all knew from personal observation, that when the ice breaks, the new crevasse is never more than a few inches wide. The initial stress causes small cracks on the surface, and only with continued strains will the cracks widen and deepen into crevasses.

The ice on which we camped was probably seven hundred feet thick. Yet it was under such a delicately balanced strain that the weight of our party of six men, three sleds, and twenty-one dogs disturbed it enough to start the breaking.

We knew all of that and nodded assent to Gould's words of comfort. Yet when we went to bed, I had trouble falling asleep. Logically, I had all the information I needed; emotionally, I wasn't so sure.

I finally dropped off. When I awakened, the bombardment had stopped. The ice had adjusted to our increased weight. By the time we repacked our sleds in the morning, the sounds had started again, probably because of our movement, but within hours we had left the area far behind us.

We experienced no further incidents like that.

———————◆———————

The return trip almost cost us Larry Gould's life. Quite early one morning, restless and unable to tolerate the confines of his sleeping bag, Gould went outside. He then violated his own strict rule against one man going out alone. He put on skis and decided to investigate the trail that lay ahead. He skied beyond the area that Mike Thorne had explored the night before.

Gould was headed straight toward the closely spaced orange flags when suddenly the snow gave way beneath him, causing him to plunge forward as he felt the surface sinking. Fortunately, the crevasse was not especially wide, so his skis caught against the walls. Slowly, cautiously, Gould dug holes in the wall of the ice and pulled himself out to safety. Then he turned and stared down at the blue-black depth of death. Fresh crevasses had opened up in the more than two months since we had set up our flags and beacons.

Our leader retraced his trail to the camp and crawled back into his sleeping bag, intending to keep quiet about the episode.

By night the air had cleared of fog, and the thin clouds promised a sun-filled night. Only then did Mike Thorne discover (and point out to us) that we had camped between two crevasses, both varying from three to twelve feet wide. Had we stopped to make camp either ten feet ahead or behind, someone would surely have fallen into the partially bridged chasms. We tried to measure the depth of one crevasse, but our longest line of two hundred fifty feet still did not touch bottom, so we could only speculate about the depth.

Minutes after our party started out, Mike Thorne turned and yelled, "Who could have been skiing out here?" He pointed to the tracks.

It didn't take us long to figure out that Larry Gould was the culprit. He neither confirmed nor denied it — but then, he didn't need to.

"He would never let *us* go out alone like this," Crockett said.

"Look!" O'Brien pointed. "What a stupid ass he was to go and jump right into that crevasse."

For days we teased him about his solitary skiing. It was better to concentrate on the humor of the situation than to think about the danger he had been in.

———————◆———————

Through our radio contacts, the people at Little America kept apprised of our travels. They also relayed news to us. On January 16, three days before our planned arrival, Byrd sent a message telling us the *New York* and the *Bolling* might not get through the exceptionally wide and thick pack ice to pick up the expedition, which was due to decamp as soon as we returned to Little America.

The next day we received word that Byrd had requested the Norwegian-owned *Nielson Alonzo* whaling factory to come to us. It would take the ship two days. He urged us to hurry.

We still had one hundred four miles ahead. Gould and I talked about pushing the dogs that far in two days—more than doubling the daily distance. Neither of us liked the idea, but we would try if we had to. The next morning Crockett got a message from Byrd just before we pushed off: The whaler could not come for us. Byrd told us not to rush.

We felt relieved. I figured we could have made the distance in two days. Those wonderful dogs would have run to their last breath for us, but it delighted me that they did not have to face that test.

————————◆————————

On January 18 we reached our last cache. We stopped only long enough to take on food supplies. The trail was easy going, and we traveled thirty-five miles that day instead of our normal twenty-three.

On January 19, we had been on the trail two hours when Thorne spotted fresh ski tracks and raced back to tell us. We thought it strange. Little America was twenty-five miles away, and we wondered why anyone would be that far from camp and alone.

Crockett smiled and pointed ahead. "That's our answer."

A figure on skis raced toward us. It was Dr. Coman. Because he did not know exactly where to meet us, he had traversed the whole area. He accompanied us the rest of the way.

When we cleared the low hills south of Little America, we spotted the radio towers pointing skyward. That view made me realize we had come home. We had covered more than fifteen hundred miles in eighty-seven days.

Though I was as eager as the others to see camp again, I didn't want the geological survey to end. I stopped my sled for a few seconds and paused long enough to turn and gaze back over our trail. Our path resembled a railroad line whose tracks grew closer and closer together.

They were the final markings of our journey, and in the end they also represented the conclusion of the era of primitive explorers. We were the last to use dogs. From then on, explorers would use planes and over-the-snow vehicles. I was sad my part was over, yet proud to have been a member of a history-making expedition.

I felt worn out but contented. We had accomplished the same feats as famous explorers like Amundsen, Scott, and Shackleton, using the same materials and under similarly harsh conditions. Our success was due not to superior equipment or technology but to better techniques and skills developed during the years between their journeys and ours.

As we started up again, I thought, it doesn't matter whether anyone writes my name down in a history book, but it does matter that I have been here. I have been a participant in the exploration of the world's last frontier — my dream come true.

My thoughts turned to Mother and Father, and I wondered whether they were as proud as I was. I touched Father's watch again as the towers grew larger.

I felt so humbled, so grateful.

Off the Ice

Word of our arrival quickly spread to everyone at Little America, and when we stopped at the radio towers, they all came out to greet us, all except George Tennant.

Gummy was busy at his stove preparing a welcome-home turkey dinner. He had acres of food spread out over the mess hall table. The six of us on the geologic team sat down first, and the table quickly filled with other revelers. Byrd had welcomed us on the ice a mile from camp, and now he joined us at the table as well.

Gummy's meal — turkey, gravy, mashed potatoes, cranberry sauce, prune bread, stuffing, and ice cream with chocolate sauce — was delicious, but we were surprised at how little we could eat. Our stomachs had shrunk, and although our taste buds were keen, we couldn't finish even our first generous helpings. Poor Gummy thought we didn't appreciate his cooking.

How we celebrated! The men gathered around the six of us, back-slapping, laughing, teasing. For a few minutes, everyone seemed to talk at once. Although we knew we had accomplished much, we were immensely gratified to hear their words of appreciation and avid expressions that we had more than fulfilled the expedition's expectations.

As much as we had liked the adventuresome spirit of the geological survey party, we were glad to be back at Little America. Under Gould's superb leadership we had experienced nothing but harmony among the six of us. Yet once we were back, I realized how much I had missed the other men. Their grinning faces and shouts of welcome made me aware of how I valued their companionship.

I thought of my school days and my parents. How pleased Father and Mother would have been to see how the group accepted us. The men didn't react as if we had merely scored the winning points in a big football game. That kind of joyousness soon fades. But they recognized that with all of us working together, we had added to the pages of history, technology, and scientific achievement.

Being twenty-five and not as mature as some of the others, I didn't appreciate at the time the lasting personal significance of membership in the Byrd expedition. I had not begun to understand that in the years ahead, no matter what else I did, I would point back to the months in the Antarctic as my finest.

One man said, "I may never do anything else in my life that anybody outside my own family cares about. But I have done one thing that gives me a place in history."

In his book, *Little America,* Byrd wrote about our return:

We gave them a royal welcome, for they had done a wonderful job. It was not the fact of having sledged 1500 miles that was remarkable. It was the fact that these men had started this punishing trip as green, from the point of view of experience, as bay trees. They went through with the dash and élan of youth. I thought that few veterans could have done as well. For the measure of the trip lay in the balancing of what was planned in advance and what was actually done: if anything, they exceeded the plans. . . . What they had endured had left its mark on their faces and bodies. They were lean, hard, grizzled and dirty. The most jovial, tattered and unwashed group of pirates that ever disgraced a quarterdeck would have blushed at the appearance of our scientists. That men could become so dirty on the tidy surface of the Barrier was incredible. . . . "A bath — and Paradise," Goodale yelled. They thronged into the mess hall, pillaging the precious pots of water which Tennant had stored for kitchen use; and as the layers of grime flaked and dissolved, we saw, as through a glass darkly, how very well and strong they looked.

With the men re-united for the first time in more than three months, we forgot for a time the uncertainty which lay over the pack ice, but not for long. Thereafter it was with us every waking hour.

———————◆———————

We had not grasped the severity of the situation at Little America. We had thought only of getting back to camp, where we could have fresh clothes, good food, and a few of the physical comforts we had missed for the past three months.

Via radio we had known about problems with the ships, but the impact didn't hit us until after we had been back at camp for several hours. Then I heard a radio message from New Zealand and a little later from the ships themselves: They could not break through the pack ice. They were idly standing by, a thousand miles away at the northern edge of the ice, waiting for the winds and ocean currents to let the ice separate enough that they could pass through.

Admiral Byrd paced the floor outside the radio shop, located in the corner of the mess hall, anxiously hearing the news from both of his ships on an hourly basis. None of the news sounded optimistic. The *City,* plowing south, met one storm after another. Three whaling factory ships, all north of the pack ice, prowled around its edge, waiting for the wind and currents to accomplish what they dared not attempt even with their powerful engines. South of the pack, two whalers, the *Nielson Alonzo* and the *Sir James Clark Ross,* waited and watched as anxiety mounted.

Byrd retained his composure, but I saw the concern and worry etched across his face. I heard him say on the radio, "Our work is done. We need to go. The men are ready and have been waiting."

Byrd tried to recruit help from any source he could think of. He sought the assistance of the Norwegian whaling fleet, pleading with the Norwegians to spare part of their fleet to break the ice from the northern side to the southern side for our ships to go through. At first they agreed, but when the *C. A. Larsen,* one of the Norwegian whaling factories, attempted to open a path for Byrd's ships, it almost got stuck itself and had to retreat as soon as the ice slacked. Byrd's ships remained stuck for two weeks. The Norwegians could not hang on indefinitely; they had to spend their time with their whale-killing business.

When Byrd told us that the ships might not get through, we immediately understood that we might have to spend another winter on the ice. No ship can get into Antarctica between February and November. Ships can approach only late in the Antarctic summer, when the belt of ice across the Ross Sea has broken up. The ice belt begins freezing solid again as soon as the round-the-clock sunshine diminishes. Once the ice freezes, ships are locked out.

We had arrived in December 1928; now it was nearing the end of January 1930. We had a month — at the most — for the ships to slip in and get us out.

As the message came over the radio, it seemed inevitable that we would spend another year on the ice. I was delighted, relishing the idea of *two* good years in Antarctica. We had no further survey trips planned, but that didn't worry me. If we stayed, Byrd would see that we would go into the field — perhaps to the Rockefeller Mountains. Gould would want more time on that range. Any plan would have pleased me: Despite Walden, it had been a wonderful year, and I had no wife or job waiting for me. In my anticipation, however, I was the exception.

Byrd must have been going through a terrible time, although he remained calm and friendly to all of us. While he and I were discussing our options, he said, "It would be a terrible thing if we had to wait here another year."

"I'd welcome the chance," I said. "I mean, I'd be happy to remain here another year. We have enough food and equipment — "

"True," he said, "but most of the men are anxious to get back. We have other commitments—families, jobs from which a further absence might mean separation papers. And remember, Bill Haines must decide which girl he's going to marry."

———————◆———————

In the midst of radio reports about the ice blockages, we had several other problems to contend with. Howard Mason, who was one of our radio operators, had been showing signs of appendicitis. Mac McKinley was also beginning to complain of similar symptoms. Although Mason was worse, neither of them was in severe pain. A third man had lost a lot of weight, his nerves were on edge, and he was miserable. Byrd feared that his already deteriorating morale could adversely affect the rest of us if we stayed.

Mason got worse. Dr. Coman stressed that if the infection progressed, he would have to operate. He didn't want to wait until the appendix burst because Mason would run the greater risk of peritonitis. So Coman prepared to perform an appendectomy in the Antarctic.

Coman set up his medical facility for surgery at a moment's notice. For an operating room he confiscated the library. Most of us joined together to scrub the walls and the wooden floor. He had a mess hall table for an operating table. With no running water, Coman did the next best thing: He prepared a number of basins with a liberal supply of disinfectant so that he could sterilize his instruments. Ever eager for new adventure, I was hoping that Coman would ask me to scrub and hand him the instruments and sutures—or at least pick up swabs from the floor.

In those days, doctors demanded complete bed rest for all surgical patients. Dr. Coman said that if he did the surgery and then the ships arrived, it would not be wise to move Mason on board. Mason would have to stay on the ice all winter.

Every day Byrd, Gould, and Coman were making and revising their contingency plans. Many factors came into play. For one thing, we would not leave the dogs behind. Nor could we take them all if a group stayed. They would need dogs. And the dogs needed me.

141

I volunteered immediately to stay, and although my offer did not surprise him, Byrd let me know he appreciated it. While not wanting the man to have any pain, I was wishing Mason's condition would deteriorate just enough so that Coman would insist on doing surgery. Dumb, maybe, but I was that exuberant.

The other two musketeers would not be with me, however. Goodale wanted to get home because a romance that started before we left had blossomed through correspondence via radio messages. He was now ready to marry.

When I suggested to Crockett that he volunteer, he said, "I don't see any reason for me to stay behind."

"You don't want to stay?" I couldn't believe his words. Immediately I gave him half a dozen reasons for not returning. "And further, how many times in life will either of us get the chance to spend another year in the Antarctic?"

Crockett smiled. "All the same, I want to go home."

In my mind, I shouted to Crockett. Wouldn't it be splendid to be left here for one more year on the Antarctic continent? We could have fresh meat from the seals and penguins. The expedition would leave sufficient supplies for everything we needed. George Tennant had volunteered to bake one hundred loaves of his delicious bread, and knowing him, he would make two hundred.

We could spend days at a time with the dogs on the ice. Most of all, I could pursue a new interest: studying the penguins. Penguins are fascinating birds, and I had fallen in love with them. I didn't learn a great deal about them because I didn't have time, but they were always around in summer. Our dogs got used to them and tolerated their presence. Had I been able to stay for another winter, I would have studied them as much as I could, especially the emperor penguins, three feet tall, who have their young in the middle of winter on the pack ice. Even if I could not get to their rookeries, which were miles away, I would hope to find a few within a safe distance from Little America. Life in Antarctica, I decided, could never be dull.

In the end, four of us volunteered to stay at the bottom of the world for another year.

———————◆———————

For days Byrd received one message after another from the ships that said, in effect, "Don't worry. We won't let you spend the winter there." In his more pessimistic moments, Byrd asked, "What if you can't do anything about it?" Most of the time he found encouragement from their promises and used that to buoy the spirits of the men anxious to leave, especially Mason.

The long-awaited message finally came: The ships were moving through the ice. They expected to be at Little America at the ice edge in four days.

Then, within a twelve-hour period, the wind shifted, and we received word that both of our ships could get through right away.

The time was so short now that the process of loading our ships and pulling out of Antarctica before getting caught in the ice ourselves was of paramount importance to Admiral Byrd.

This urgency intensified the decision-making moment for Dr. Coman. He decided that the appendectomy did not have to be performed. The inflammation was going down. Mason's general health was good, and he was successfully fighting the infection. Coman thought if Mason didn't take a sudden turn for the worse, he could make it until he reached New Zealand — and that's what eventually happened.

I was crushed to think that I'd have to go back. But once I acknowledged that the decision was out of my hands, I had so much to do, I forgot my disappointment. Alongside the other dog men I worked furiously, taking things from Little America to the ice edge, ready to be loaded as soon as the ships arrived.

When we were awaiting their arrival, Mac McKinley, forever relieved of his secret mission, took charge of demobilizing Little America. He faced the problem of where to haul the goods we were taking back. He decided on a spot Byrd had named Floyd Bennett Bay. If both the *City* and the *Bolling* reached the Bay of Whales, we would simply load both ships. If only one ship made it through — which would be the *City*, since the *Bolling* was made of steel — then came the difficulty of selection because we would be taking fewer things back.

Byrd identified the things that he wanted taken on the ship, carefully allocating the space available. When I first thought about the situation, it seemed silly to worry about space. We had brought six hundred fifty tons of food and equipment to Antarctica. In a year we had eaten most of the food, and we were abandoning the buildings and going back with fewer animals. Yet Byrd found it difficult to decide exactly what we should include. He seemed to change his mind every other day about some of the equipment.

We couldn't take everything back. We also faced the risk of transporting heavy equipment to the edge of the ice. At any time the ice might break off and float away. Finally Byrd, being a fine administrator, designated everything A, B, or C. *A* items included records and valuable scientific equipment. *B* and *C* were progressively less valuable materials. When Byrd had his list completed, it still left out tons of equipment, food, clothing, fuel, and of course, housing. We piled the *A* items one mile from the ice edge, ready to move them forward the moment the ships arrived.

The *Bolling* reached the northern edge of the pack ice on January 29, but it could not break through. For twenty-four hours the ship battled the wrath of nature and finally, defeated, turned northward and never made it.

That answered one crucial question: We would load as much as we could on the *City . . . if she got through.*

On the last day of January a heavy storm descended on us and blanketed the whole camp. February snaked in, dark and gloomy, reminding us of the impending winter. The sky was already darkening at night. Cold winds blew in from the south. The sea beat against the barrier cliffs to the north. Although miles away, we could hear its powerful waves striking.

Byrd spent sleepless days and nights near the radio, and on February 7, 1930, we got the welcome news that the *City* had cut through the pack ice. For three days she had bucked the ice only to have to run to escape a heavy gale. The ship steamed on when the storm abated and encountered another terrible storm.

The tightly packed ice interlocked with immense bergs. In places, the crew estimated, the crust reached a thickness of twenty feet. On at least two occasions the *City* barely wriggled from a dangerous squeeze. Icebergs, with seven eighths of their volume below the surface, were propelled through the pack ice by underwater currents. The weather turned so cold that ice accumulated on the decks, masts, and rigging faster than the men could chop it away. The prow of the ship began to sink under the weight. The men worked with superhuman effort, but the ice kept gaining on them. Ice, some one hundred fifty tons of it, was sinking the ship.

The wind stiffened, bringing snow squalls and cold. The captain feared he would have to turn about and run with it. Determined to reach us, he stubbornly pressed on.

As the Ross Sea turned ever angrier, the wind stiffened to full hurricane force, with gusts exceeding one hundred miles per hour. The ship met the storm head-on. The gale lasted twenty-four hours, yet somehow the ship stayed afloat. The following afternoon, the sea calmed somewhat: The *City* kept going and the crews kept chopping. The Ross Sea was choked for twenty miles with new ice blown from the south bays, and the ship had immense difficulty traversing it.

For more than a week, each sudden clearing was followed by a fresh storm and the renewed fear of ice blockage. On February 15 the exhausted crew was ready to give up when the lookout spotted Mount Erebus, an active volcano. Then the crew sighted Ross Island. The winds had driven them more than three hundred miles off course.

While the ship battled to get to us, we did not remain idle. By Sunday, February 16, we had moved everything to Floyd Bennett Bay and laid it out in three distinct piles. Half the men were living there, waiting for the ship. The carpenters made a mess hall out of dog crates and used an overturned ski from the Ford plane for a table. We had two lines of tents facing each other with tons of gear piled between them.

The next day, the *City* radioed us that it had sighted the Bay of Whales. Within minutes, the men at Bennett Bay spotted the *City*. The ship had taken forty-four days to travel a distance of twenty-four hundred miles — and had spent six weeks battling ice packs, storms, and high seas.

Within six hours of her arrival, the radio station at Little America signed off forever.

In the meantime we started hauling the *A* materials aboard ship. The camp at Floyd Bennett Bay was about a mile from Little America. As we moved back and forth, reversing our work of a year earlier, the trail wound back and forth around the pressure ridges. We found it no easier than before, but we kept on.

Our dog teams rushed between the hastily stacked supplies and the ship as hard as they could. One driver, who had worked around the clock before the ship arrived, got so tired he could not make another trip, even though the dogs were still willing to go on. Another man replaced him for ten hours, and the dog team worked right through the night. The first man, now fully rested, went back to work with lighter loads but driving the same dogs.

We loaded the ship as fast as we could and finished in just under thirty-six hours. The ship kept up its steam, the booms and winches were working, and the men were yelling, screaming, and loading. The captain, anxious to shove off, would wait only until we had everything on board and not one minute longer. Finally the last cargo was loaded: our dogs.

About nine o'clock on the morning of February 19, 1930, Captain Melville gave the order, which the crewmen on deck repeated, "Cast off!" Within minutes the ship was nosing her way through the loose ice in the Bay of Whales and plowing seaward.

I had thought that once on board the ship, I would be more willing to go, but I shed a lot of internal tears about leaving. I said to myself, I'll never get back here again; I'll never have another chance like this again, not ever in my whole life.

Gazing back at the ice, I whispered, "I loved it there. I wish I could have stayed."

Then I thought of the breathtaking adventures I had had since becoming involved with Richard Byrd. The past two years had been absolutely wonderful. I had come to the ice a kid, partway through college. I felt that I went home a man, seasoned by experience and danger.

And then I remembered my final minutes at Little America. As Mac McKinley lowered the colors for the last time, Byrd and I stood at attention. Had the other two men not been with me, I suspect I would have burst into tears.

On the last load from Little America to the ship, I carried Admiral Byrd on my sled. As he got off, he looked at me and said simple words that expressed my feelings, too: "It's over, Norman."

I nodded. I had a hundred things I wanted to say, and yet no words seemed to come.

Byrd took a few steps, paused, and turned back. Flashing his engaging smile, he said, "We did it. Now we must celebrate our victory."

I forced myself not to look back down the trail. I wanted to forget my disappointment, but feelings much like those I had had years earlier when leaving home for boarding school came over me. Even if we should return, nothing would be the same as it had been the past sixteen months. Silently, I said good-bye to a fearsome but majestic continent.

Home

Standing on the deck of the *City*, unsure of my emotions, I kept my eyes glued to the sea. As soon as we were away from the ice, Antarctica showed its most beautiful side. The sun's rays lit up the barrier cliffs, bringing out lovely blue and purple hues.

I overheard Byrd say to McKinley, "Another week, I think, and we would have been there to stay—at least until another year had passed."

I sighed. Too late to go back. I joined the other men in securing the decks and making certain our dog crates were lashed and nailed. We would open these boxes three times a day to feed, water, and exercise our animals.

The belt of pack ice was loose when we reached it, and we pushed through without difficulty. I climbed up into the crow's-nest along with Sverre Strom to watch the seals and penguins dive as we passed by. They were resting and sunning themselves on our course. Having probably never seen a ship before, they waited until the last moment before they moved. This last-minute activity gave Strom and me a good look at their swimming maneuvers under water.

The first night we were on board, the *City* began to roll. Every one of our forty stomachs became squeamish. Several men actually got seasick. One of our number who had traveled the seas often and had never suffered seasickness before fared no better than the rest of us. He insisted that the cook had served something poisonous in the food. Yet the food did not cause our upset stomachs.

Our bodies must have become quiet and regular after more than a year ashore. We had had no automobiles or elevators, and only a handful of men had flown in the plane. Therefore, the slightest roll upset our sense of balance. By the second day, we had adjusted to the rolling of the ship and had no more trouble.

———————◆———————

On February 27, a whaler, *Kosmos,* came alongside us, and we transferred Mason and McKinley to that ship. The *Kosmos* traveled faster and got them to Dunedin ahead of us.

On March 10, we landed at Dunedin. As we stepped off the ship, Byrd gave each of us one hundred dollars. Most of the men headed for a bar. Not being a drinker and having no special needs, I had time to look around the city. On my previous trip, the job of mixing dog food had confined me almost the entire time to Hudson Brothers Chocolate Factory. It took most of the morning to get used to seeing lots of people and houses and hearing the sounds of civilization once again.

In one store a herringbone topcoat grabbed my attention. Made of New Zealand wool and priced at sixty dollars, it was the most beautifully woven garment I had ever seen. I bought the coat, which lasted me many years.

We stayed in New Zealand for ten days. Out of eagerness to get the dogs through the equatorial zone as quickly as possible, Crockett, Goodale, and I shipped out on another whaling vessel, the *C. A. Larsen.* Walden and his Chinooks were on board, too. His Norwegian friends had told me that while I was out with the geological party, he had calmed down, and indeed, the intensity of his animus toward me seemed to have moderated. He and I even spoke, albeit in formal terms. And one day when he was feeling ill, he allowed me to carry water to his dogs. Still, I remained watchful.

The *Larsen* took us straight across the Pacific, through the Panama Canal, and directly to New York Harbor. This time, I did not volunteer for the black gang.

————————◆————————

When the *Larsen* tied up at dock in New York, Mother was there, along with several family members and friends. I felt safe and secure, just seeing her waving to me as I disembarked. Father had stayed at home to prepare for my arrival, or more accurately, the arrival of my dogs.

While still on the ice, I had asked whether anyone wanted a dog when we got back to the States. Nearly half the men said, "I sure do." Each one named the animal he wanted.

But by the time we reached New Zealand, they had changed their minds. Mike Thorne was the exception. His sister met the ship in New York, and she picked up Dinty. (Walden, of course, was inseparable from his Chinooks; he shipped them out by train straight to New Hampshire.)

Taking care of the other dogs then fell on my shoulders. Keeping them would be a problem, but I was pleased at the prospect of having them with me. I had wired my father, and he agreed that I could bring them home to our farm in Hamilton, Massachusetts.

The farm already had twenty cows, a couple of draft horses, and pigs and chickens. Now there would be fifty-four dogs in addition. Inevitably, some would get loose and kill the chickens or chase the milch cows. So while I was catching up on family news with Mother, Father was fencing in a yard and preparing crates and leashes.

On our way home in the train I devised a plan by which the dogs could earn their keep. Sensing that people were extremely curious about the expedition and assuming that we participants would remain news for several months, I decided to put up a gate and allow tourists to view the huskies who had lived and worked with us in Antarctica. Visitors would pay twenty-five cents each for the opportunity.

I never got around to putting my plan into effect. For one thing, only two weeks after I had arrived home, Goodale and Crockett and I went back to New York with our families to meet the expedition ships and to enjoy the privilege of being in an open-car parade through Manhattan. We musketeers were in the second car with Larry and Peggy Gould, right behind Admiral and Mrs. Byrd, Bernt Balchen, Mac McKinley, and Harold June — they had all been Byrd's crew on the polar flight. New York police and military guards escorted us, and a U.S. Navy marching band preceded us.

On Wall Street we experienced a real ticker-tape parade. As our car crept along, I looked upward at an amazing sight. Between the tall buildings, paper floated down in such wild abundance, it looked like a snowstorm. People in other buildings on the parade route showered pages from telephone directories and the contents of circular files, but the Wall Street tape was the most thrilling.

Back home, even though I hadn't promoted the dogs, there was a constant flow of visitors and of letters and phone calls from people who wanted to come and take pictures of my well-traveled huskies. My parents never said anything, but I could tell they were discomforted. So after four months, when Eddie Goodale decided that he wanted the dogs on his family's farm, I was happy to let him take them. There he borrowed my entrepreneurial idea. He charged twenty-five cents a visit and fifty cents at four in the afternoon, when the dogs received their daily feeding. For another fifty cents, visitors could feed the dogs themselves. In that way Goodale made a living for several months.

When winter came and the tourist business slacked off, the two of us went backpack camping in New Hampshire, mostly around Mount Washington. After that we skied every weekend. In the winter of 1932 I collected pictures and information on skiing and published the first book on skiing in the United States. Its title, *Ski Fever,* proved prophetic, and I sold some three thousand copies.

Naturally, my parents expected me to go back to college. After my great adventure on the ice, college seemed boring. Deep within I sensed that I would never go back to a classroom again; I had changed too much. But rather than admit that to my parents, I said, "I'm not ready to go back now."

Goodale and Crockett never returned to Harvard, either. We were too excited about living in the aftermath of the expedition. Almost every day we picked up newspaper accounts of our work in Antarctica.

From these stories I learned why Byrd had made us promise not to publish anything about the expedition for one year. According to the papers, he was badly in debt—one hundred and twenty-five thousand dollars. From the sale of his book, *Little America,* he was hoping to net enough in royalties at one dollar a copy to pay off the debts of the expedition. Eventually, he did.

———————◆———————

In addition to appointing Byrd to the rank of rear admiral (ret.) while we were still in Antarctica, Congress issued a special Congressional Medal of Honor for all of those on the expedition recommended by Byrd and Gould. Instead of making a single group presentation, Byrd visited each of us individually and awarded the medals.

One day Byrd phoned me. "Norman, I'm going to visit John D. Rockefeller at his home in Maine. Could you drive up to Maine and meet me? I'd like to have you come with me."

Naturally I agreed. My curiosity to meet the famous Rockefeller would have been enough of an incentive. But again, when an invitation came from Byrd, it seemed like a command, although I doubt he meant it that way. I drove all night and met Byrd in Camden, Maine. The admiral was friendly and cordial, and we chatted a few minutes. Knowing how tired I was, he insisted on driving so that I could sleep during most of the next two hours' drive to the Rockefeller mansion.

Rockefeller had faithfully supported the expedition from the time of the announcement, for which Byrd had showed his appreciation by naming a mountain range after him on his first flight upon arriving in Antarctica. He and Balchen had flown the Fairchild in late January 1929 over the area. Byrd referred to this discovery in his book:

For a time the peaks of this range danced across my vision, gradually growing smaller while the bare rock diminished to mere pin points, and I found myself wondering what we should name it. The names of several of the men who had befriended the expedition came to my mind; and foremost among these was that of John D. Rockefeller, Jr. And it occurred to me that his true inner life is as little known as those peaks which we had just seen. His character is in keeping with that of these austere mountain masses. He stands, steady as a rock, in the chaos of life, and the great power he controls is directed wisely and unselfishly for the betterment of the world.

I could do no better than to name this range after him — Rockefeller Mountains.

I had my first view of the famous millionaire when Byrd and I walked up the wide wooden steps so popular in those Maine summer houses. Rockefeller came outside, and we met on the large veranda.

The two men, who had known each other for years, greeted each other with handshakes and warm tones. Rockefeller was, as I had seen in photographs, rather thin and old, but he had a surprising vitality about him. He referred to the admiral as Dick — the only person I ever heard call Byrd by that name.

Byrd introduced the old man to me as J. D., and both of us addressed him that way during our visit.

J. D. invited us into his dining room. It was a big room with a high ceiling; I noticed a large rectangular table with high-backed chairs. The table was bare except for flowers in the center. J. D. led us past the table to a bay window that overlooked his harbor. He pointed out his yacht, which was tied to a float.

"Beautiful view," I commented.

"I like gazing at the water," he said. "It's so peaceful."

I saw a smaller table, set for six. Immediately a butler pulled out J. D.'s chair, waited until he was seated, and then pushed the chair back in. Gracefully he moved behind the chair on J. D.'s right and pulled it back for Byrd.

J. D. said to me, "Would you sit here?" He pointed to the chair on his left. I seated myself before the butler got to me.

The breakfast of orange juice, eggs, bacon, milk, toast, and coffee passed too quickly. The conversation between Byrd and J. D. was friendly, and they spoke with ease to each other.

I had a momentary insight into the greatness of Rockefeller because he paused from time to time and addressed questions to me, the kind of questions that made me think he actually cared about the answers. His interest and friendliness made me feel at home with the two of them.

After breakfast we walked into J. D.'s immense library. A stone fireplace broke up the pattern of filled shelves around the room. J. D. walked over to the mantel and picked up the box that contained my special Congressional Medal. Byrd stood next to him, and they faced me. J. D. made an appropriate statement, but I was so nervous I couldn't remember the words three minutes later. He paused, opened the box, took out the medal with its long ribbon, and placed it over my head.

"The admiral told me you deserved this medal and I'm glad to present it to you with my thanks." He shook my hand; the strength of his grip amazed me. Then he handed me an envelope that came with the medal. The envelope contained a one-page commendation from Congress.

The ceremony over, we sat down in the library, and the two men talked about Maine and the fog that had held cruising down for a week. The New York Yacht Club Cruise, which Rockefeller planned to host, was due to start that afternoon if the fog lifted.

Rockefeller paused, turned to me, and smiled. "It is my greatest contribution and personal satisfaction to support Dick and the expedition that he led. You should be proud to belong to Byrd."

"I am, sir," I said. "Very proud." And I could think of no time when I had felt any prouder.

———————◆———————

We spent two hours with Rockefeller before we drove to Byrd's house on an island in Penobscot Bay, Maine. He didn't ask me to spend the night, so I drove back to Boston, where I was then working.

Byrd and I stayed in contact. He phoned me occasionally at first, and then more frequently. In the few instances when I phoned him, he never refused to take the call, and his voice always conveyed the idea that he considered it a privilege to talk to me.

Several times I visited his house, and once he invited me to spend the night there. Byrd and I had a warm relationship; I wouldn't call it intimate. The admiral knew many people, and he was already a world-famous figure. Yet Byrd did not have intimate friends. He simply wasn't that kind of man, even though he genuinely liked people and they respected him. While the admiral reserved a special place in his heart for those of us who went to the ice with him, the relationship with any of us was what I would call "warmly distant."

In 1935, after the birth of my son, Byrd sent him a silver porringer engraved with his full name: Gerard Gould Vaughan. Below that was the date and "From R. E. B."

In the months after our return, I realized how deeply he cared about the men who went to Antarctica with him. Word soon circulated that Byrd was known as a soft touch for those who had been on the expedition. The admiral insisted that without us he could not have achieved his goals.

I never asked Byrd for favors. As I learned, that was not true of some of the men. Several asked him for money, others for assistance in buying a home. One member even asked him to cosign a note on an airplane.

After Antarctica

$\mathbf{B}$ack at home again, I talked over my future with my parents. Already sure of not wanting to return to Harvard, I didn't want to disappoint them again. After hedging a few minutes I finally told them.

"Norman, if you don't want to return," Mother said, "your decision disappoints us, but we'll respect your wish."

It must have been hard for her to say that to me. Although Mother never actually said so, my going to Harvard meant a lot to her. She very much wanted me to graduate, yet she loved me enough not to impose her desires on me.

"Things are better for me outside of college," I said. "I just can't go back into an academic atmosphere again."

"What will you do?" my father asked. For him, that was the major question.

"Go to work, like everybody else," I said.

That's exactly what I did. Within days I started my business career by selling advertising space in *Time* and *The Sportsman*. Although successful at the job, I found the work so dull I turned to an advertising agency.

I knew a number of people in the advertising business, so I contacted them. One friend worked with N. W. Ayer and Son of Philadelphia, and I asked for his help. I chose N. W. Ayer because it was the largest ad agency in the world, based on the dollar volume spent for its clients. The company had its own printing plant for preparing advertisements, booklets, and promotional material.

My friend went to the head office in Philadelphia and asked the people in charge of hiring to look me over. "I'm convinced that he's a man with a future in the advertising business," he told them. They must have thought so, too, because a week later they interviewed me and hired me on the same day.

The Ayer company groomed me for the management position of account executive. But first my employers insisted that I gain experience in every department in the Philadelphia office. After a month of learning the system in one section, they moved me to another area. By the time I had been through every department, I had functioned as a glorified messenger boy, but I had also grasped how the company worked. Each job fitted into the whole picture.

To get a little financial boost (I came back from Little America penniless) I tried out for Philadelphia's semipro football team and made the team. I loved the game and had tried out unsuccessfully for the Harvard team. The semipro team gave me a chance to do what I loved — and get expenses paid as well.

This seemed an ideal arrangement. I worked for the Ayer company during the day and had my real fun at night. The team practiced two evenings a week, and we played on Sundays.

On the Monday after a Sunday game, a department head in N. W. Ayer called me to his office. He stared at me silently and then asked, "Norman, do you want to be an account executive for us?"

"Yes, sir," I said.

"Is that what you really want?"

"Of course," I said. "I'm learning all I can by moving from one department to another. Isn't my work satisfactory?"

"No complaints regarding your work," he said. "However, I want you to understand something. An account executive has to have a clean face—a good face. We don't want a man who represents N. W. Ayer to have a marred-up face."

He paused, but I must have been a little slow because I sat in stony silence, trying to figure out what he meant.

"Any man in a responsible position must be physically acceptable," he said. "A man with our company can't have anything the matter with him."

Still having no idea what he was driving at, I protested, "I'm in good condition. In fact, I'm in top shape and—"

He waved my words aside and peered directly at me. "If you continue to play football you're going to end up with a broken nose, a cut face, or some other terrible injury. In that case, you would no longer be acceptable to us."

I stared in disbelief. I wondered what kind of football he had been watching. Of course, such things were possible and they did happen, but I certainly didn't expect to become beat-up and broken. Right or wrong, he gave me an ultimatum: Quit football or quit Ayer.

Although I was eager to play ball, I had to make my way in the business world. I said, "I understand. I'll resign from the team immediately."

Throwing myself into the work at Ayer, I tried hard to make good. In terms of results, my work was good. But life, I decided, was more than results. It took six months before my downcast mind finally admitted, I'm stuck with a bunch of businessmen who don't appreciate the outdoors. When I refer to Antarctica, they haven't the slightest idea why anyone would want to go there. Their only interest in sports lies in watching professional games or listening to them on the radio (this was long before television).

Until then I had been around people who liked being outdoors, and while they might not want to go to Antarctica themselves, they appreciated my desire to go. Most of my friends enjoyed hunting, fishing, canoeing, hiking, and just being outside and involving themselves with nature. But not the people I found myself working with.

"We speak a different language," I said to myself one day.

I must have gone into a kind of depression. I felt closed in all the time. I ran around opening windows, wanting to breathe the fresh air. I boarded with a family that rented to young professional men. During the summer, I slept on the lawn most nights. They thought I was a little peculiar. I'm sure I was. They couldn't understand why I preferred to sleep outside. When no one could understand my love for the outdoors, I sank further into myself.

Living in a metropolitan area, most of the people I knew or worked with saw only the joys of city living, the conveniences, the concrete buildings and places of amusement. I finally found one acceptable way to throw off the city's confinement. After work and on weekends, I hurried out of Philadelphia and raced toward the beach at Atlantic City. Once there, I walked alone on the beach for hours.

Soon life became a matter of endurance. My one chance for any peace of mind and for open spaces came in returning to New England. When he hired me, the personnel director had indicated that once I learned the job and had some practical experience, the company would consider transferring me. That one hope kept me going. If I can get back to New England, I told myself every day, I'll be able to get more involved with nature again.

Six months later, I got my promotion and a transfer to Boston.

My transfer to Boston came automatically because top management knew I had come from that area. My friends in the Ayer organization were in Boston, and they requested that I join them as an account executive. I received a position with the small accounts. It required being on the road and doing a lot of investigating in the field.

The first thing I did after renting an apartment in Boston was to visit Goodale. I asked him for six dogs — which he gladly gave me — so that I could have my own team again. He let me keep them at his home and pick them up whenever I could get away. My mind was already planning for winter, when I could take the dogs and go sledding. Just having the animals helped me a lot. Spending time with them kept my mind off missing Antarctica.

On weekends I began driving dogs seriously and entered my team in the New England Sled Dog Club races.

In the winter of 1932, I participated in a particularly important dogsled event, the qualifying race for the U.S. Olympic team. I won, which made the occasion even more exciting. The win enabled me to represent the United States in the 1932 Olympics at Lake Placid, New York. Interestingly, this was the only year the Olympics featured dogsled racing as an event.

I arrived in Lake Placid in February 1932, less than a week before the actual race. The limited time forced me to spend every possible minute with my dogs. I didn't have a handler. Working with the dogs meant not being able to visit the bobsled course or watch the hockey play-offs or observe the figure skating. I didn't mind; I concentrated on being with my animals.

My dogs and I raced twenty-five miles a day for three days. I didn't win a medal. In fact, I came in very poorly, placing tenth. Not winning didn't bother me because I raced for the pure sport of it. I loved moving along with my dogs and the feeling of togetherness with them. Just racing across the land gave me more pleasure than anything else.

The Olympic experience was over before I realized it. I returned in a freight car with my dogs. The next day meant wearing my suit, talking advertising, and living my old way of life. *And I hated it.*

———◆———

During this period, I learned to hitchhike. As well as saving me money, hitchhiking provided adventure and added a touch of excitement to my life. In those days we hitchhiked safely, and none of us ever heard of any foul play. I went to Boston from Philadelphia, traveling through New York City by subway because I quickly learned that people only offer rides along the highway.

On one trip, late at night, I was not getting any lifts, so I climbed up the ladder on the rear of a bus that had stopped at a light and snuggled down among the baggage carried on the roof. I thought of it as a lark and was enjoying myself immensely. The night was already overcast, but

within a few miles the rain started and pelted me. Luckily, I had prepared for bad weather. From my pack, I opened my folded-up raincoat.
The wind whipped it right out of my hands. In amazement, I watched
the coat flapping like a bird as the wind carried it off the roof. Not being
particularly bothered about getting wet, I hunkered down under the
luggage as best I could. The trip was turning out to be more fun than I
had expected.

By the time the bus reached Hartford the rain had stopped, but it
didn't matter to me because my soggy clothes couldn't have held any
more water anyway. The bus stopped at the depot and the driver climbed
up to get a bag for a departing passenger. He saw me, paused a second,
and descended quickly without a word. My heart was pounding, and I
was plain scared. After all, I was doing something illegal. When nothing
more happened after a few seconds, I assumed that he had decided to
ignore me.

Another two minutes passed, and hearing voices, I peered over the
side. Half a dozen people on the sidewalk stared up at me. The passen-
gers had come out of the bus to witness what they assumed was a
robbery. I stared dumbly at them, not sure what to do. A policeman
arrived and made the decision for me.

Gun in hand, he ordered me to come down. I had no escape. "Over
there," he growled. He pushed me up against the wall of the terminal,
making me keep my hands above my head. After a search produced no
gun or knife, the driver went up to the roof to look for my weapons. He
came down minutes later, empty-handed, and reported, "No cut or
ripped bags."

I was still standing against the wall, my hands held high, trying to
explain. "I was only hitchhiking. I wouldn't steal anything." With my
soaked clothes and a dirty face (which I didn't discover until later), I
must have looked horrible.

"Driver," the policeman asked, ignoring me, "do you want to come to
the station and press charges?"

"No, I guess not," he answered. "It would take too long."

Relieved, I assumed the policeman was going to let me go. He did
let me put my hands down. "Just stand right there and don't move," he

said. I wondered then if he was going to take me to the police station anyway.

The bus reloaded and took off. A few curious onlookers remained. Once the bus was out of sight, the officer said, "All right, young fellow, you leave town now. And you leave without asking for a ride."

"Yes, sir," I said, delighted to get away from him. He had a patrol car but didn't offer to help me. As I started to walk away, he yelled, "If you go about half a mile, you'll come to a bridge. Then you'll be out of my jurisdiction."

For the first time I smiled, and I waved thanks as I trudged off.

The first morning on my new job in Boston, I met Iris Rodey, secretary to the office manager. She was twenty-five, pretty, and dark complexioned with reddish-blonde hair. One of the smartest people I ever met, and far smarter than I, Iris loved working with the advertising agency and was a model of efficiency. She not only managed the office but also functioned as secretary to the senior account executive.

I liked Iris the first time we met and soon invited her to dinner. We had a fine time and enjoyed each other's company. From then on Iris and I started going out together regularly. After falling in love, we decided to get married.

After a year and a half of marriage, Iris took a leave of absence from work and gave birth to our son, whom we named Gerard Gould Vaughan; the middle name was for my wonderful friend from the expedition days, Dr. Laurence McKinley Gould. Larry wrote that he was honored. Over the years he has been genial and close to Jerry, whom he likes very much.

Like a good businessman, I was following the acceptable steps upward. My sales record impressed my employers. Iris and I continued to live in Boston. Everything was going smoothly. But I was still unhappy.

I know now that I liked driving dogs better than anything else in the world. But dogsledding wasn't a respectable position in those days. The sport paid no money, so I was forced to work to support my passion; still,

I was away from home with my dogs too often. I also liked to hunt and fish, which again meant more time away from home. Iris didn't complain, even though she had no desire to join me in any of these activities. We had recognized our different interests when we married. But we were in love and foolishly believed that our love would be strong enough to keep us happy. But it was not.

I had become a loner. My return to the normal work world was a terrific letdown. I experienced some of the same feelings years later when I returned to civilian life after being in the Air Force, mostly in the Arctic, during World War II.

I couldn't talk to people about Antarctica because I felt they didn't understand how deeply it had affected me. I liked the hard, physically demanding life. I couldn't get used to social activities, especially parties where people stood around and did nothing but talk and drink. I found myself irritated at having to do the expected things.

I did go to social functions and had a good time while there. I always knew a lot of people in attendance. By nature I'm gregarious, and I mix well. But I dreaded going and tried to find reasons not to attend. When we got home, I'd wonder why I went.

I began to feel tied down, as if I had lost my freedom. I preferred nature over the city. I liked being with my dogs in places where I didn't shave or bathe for a week and lived off my own version of hoosh. My stubborn and incurable longing for the outdoors and for adventure has made me a difficult man to live with.

I tried to accommodate Iris, and I knew I was hurting her because she could not understand my need to be alone, my jumping to go mushing every chance I had. I loved her, but I realized that that emotion was not enough. When Jerry was born, my struggle grew even more intense. I felt that every time I went hunting or sledding with my dogs, I was neglecting my family. Drained emotionally, I found myself fighting bouts of depression.

"Something has to change," I said again and again. I wasn't being fair to Iris or to my son. I loathed my terrible behavior, my selfishness, yet being in the open with my dogs brought the only pleasure — and peace — I knew in those days.

Adjustments

$\mathbf{M}$y conversations with Richard Byrd continued, and I enjoyed them immensely. He was a link not only to a past that I treasured but also to a life without any encumbrances.

After my move to Boston, Byrd invited me to travel with him several times when he lectured. If the places were close enough to my job, I went.

I think Byrd wanted me to go primarily as an exhibit—and I don't mean he felt condescending toward me. Byrd wanted my presence as part of the living proof that he used in telling people of the days on the ice. In the first section of the lecture, Byrd would introduce me and ask me to stand. Then he would say, "This young man went with us to Antarctica. He voluntarily left Harvard to train sled dogs and eventually was in charge of the dogs which made our expedition click." He would ask me to say a few words about a particular event.

He sometimes invited Goodale as well, and the three of us traveled all through New England. The most memorable event together was a crowded lecture at Boston's Statler Hotel.

Paul Siple, a Boy Scout representative and the youngest man on the expedition, brought to Boston four of the twelve emperor penguins Byrd had transported from Antarctica. Goodale and I arranged for their care at the Statler. We had five loads of block ice brought in from the Boston Ice Company and deposited on the stage. We had to keep the birds happy, and that required ice.

The hotel manager, when he learned what we were doing, went wild with anxiety and outrage. "The ice will melt. You'll flood the whole place!"

"Nothing like that will happen," I explained calmly. It would take days for the large blocks of ice to melt. As it melted, water flowed onto a waterproof canvas. Goodale and I had mops ready. We soaked up the water, squeezed it into buckets, and dumped it down a drain at the back of the stage. We had no real problem, and the manager's anxiety and wrath subsided.

We built a wall with these blocks of ice and surrounded it with paneled curtains. We added movable screens, seven feet high, in such a way that they kept the penguins in one section, close enough to the front for everyone to see them when the time came. Goodale and I sat on chairs behind a large curtain while Byrd addressed the crowd from the rostrum.

The penguins cooperated beautifully by not making noise. Paul Siple fed them dead fish until Byrd wanted to show them. Siple would have loved to feed them live fish, which was impossible, but we had herring that varied from four to nine inches. The birds didn't object and ate them willingly. But that was because Paul Siple had trained them. When the penguins first reached America, they wouldn't eat anything but live fish.

Finally, Byrd said, "You are now going to enjoy seeing Antarctic penguins. This is the first time they have ever been publicly shown to an audience in the United States of America."

The curtains parted, and the crowd ecstatically clapped and rose to their feet. The penguins stood there as if trying to figure out what was going on. Siple, Goodale, and I guarded the front of the three-sided barricade of ice blocks to keep the penguins from wandering as the audience gave Byrd an ovation.

Then we stepped behind the curtain and Admiral Byrd remained in front of the penguins, talking and keeping an eye on the unpredictable birds. We watched from our position, ready to spring into action if needed. The penguins remained quietly on the ice during the next twenty minutes of Byrd's show.

When I wanted to go with Byrd on these occasional speaking engagements, I would tell my employer, "Admiral Byrd would like me to go with him to New York," or whatever city he had scheduled for his meetings.

"Of course, Norman," my employer would say without the slightest hesitation. Perhaps he thought my going and being introduced as an employee of N. W. Ayer provided excellent publicity for the company. Or perhaps he consented because it was Byrd who wanted me. Whatever the reason, he let me go, and I felt honored that Byrd was asking me.

Only gradually did Goodale and I feel we truly were linked to Byrd by our common bond of being in Antarctica together. Byrd often said, "I am proud to have you on the stage with me." We thought at the time he was just being nice. For a long time we didn't realize how deeply committed Byrd felt toward those whom he called his loyal friends.

Over the following months, because of Byrd's kind words, his frequent contacts, and his obvious interest in our lives, we began to understand that we were indeed friends of Richard Byrd.

At home Iris and I seemed to find a multitude of things to differ over, which led to constant arguments. At work I was doing quite well for the company, but I was not happy. What else should I do? That question came to me often. While a part of me kept trying to tell myself that I would eventually adjust, I don't think I ever did.

Then a significant telephone call from Byrd in 1933 changed everything for me.

"Norman, I'm going back to the South Pole next year," he said. "I'd like to have you go with me." Quite matter-of-factly, as if he planned a trip across the state, Byrd laid out details. I don't recall exactly how the conversation went, but I became as excited as I had been in 1928 when I heard about the first expedition. This time perhaps more so, because I knew what to expect. For months I had eagerly waited for something to change in my life. Now Byrd was handing me just that opportunity.

"I'd love to go," I said. He had no idea how badly I wanted to go back to Antarctica.

"I don't know about your family situation. How disruptive would this expedition be?"

"I can work that out," I said.

"The people at Ayer have generously given you time off to assist in my lectures, but will they give you this much time off?"

"I think so," I said. I had already made up my mind that I would go. If going on the expedition meant having to find another job afterward, that seemed a small price to pay.

As it turned out, the N. W. Ayer company granted me a year's leave of absence. I was free to go, and my employers would have a job waiting for me when I got back — if I still wanted to work for them.

Once I agreed to the 1934 expedition, Byrd told me, "We've already started getting things together at the Boston Navy Yard." Obviously he had been thinking about this project for a long time and had done a lot of preliminary work before contacting me.

Then Byrd told me where he wanted me to fit into his plans. "Would you be willing to solicit equipment for the expedition? You already know most of what we'll need."

"Of course," I said. "I could do that job." I was delighted to take on the role. Without exaggeration, it was a heavy responsibility and one that would have a powerful effect on the outcome of the expedition. I responded with confidence that I could handle such an assignment.

"I would never have asked you, Norman," Byrd said, "if I didn't have absolute faith in your ability."

From that moment on, anytime Byrd referred to the 1934 expedition, it was in terms of "we." He would say, "Norman, we need a good radio operator," or "This time we must make more use of air power."

A few days later he telephoned with an announcement. "Norman, we have help for you. Victor Czegka has agreed to work with us. He won't be going with us to Antarctica, but he is eager to help us prepare for the expedition." Byrd would raise the money; Victor and I would get the equipment.

Victor Czegka was then working at the naval yard. We had seen each other a number of times after we came back to the States and had become good friends. The bond of our months in Antarctica had overcome his hatred of dog men. A year after our return, Victor married and I was honored to be best man at his wedding.

Victor was not only a genius with his machines and tools, but I learned that he was also a genuinely fine man. We had relatively few differences during the next nine months as we worked together. I had left Ayer and was working full-time for the second expedition.

Byrd's plans to go back to the South Pole seemed to the so-called experts to be a matter of bad timing. They pointed out that the severe economic depression engulfing America made it difficult to solicit funds or equipment. Byrd announced his intentions nevertheless. He appealed primarily to those moguls of industry who hardly felt the effects of a depression. Rockefeller came through again. Edsel Ford and other backers of the 1929 expedition pledged generously. At one point I know Byrd had one hundred fifty thousand dollars in the treasury — a lot of money in those days.

On this Antarctic trip Byrd planned to study the wide expanse of the unknown land east of New Zealand's claim — between the Rockefeller Mountains and the Palmer Peninsula. Byrd also sincerely believed that someday America would officially acknowledge the newly discovered area. Doing additional exploration and investigation would strengthen our nation's claim.

He wanted to use the *City of New York* and the *Eleanor Bolling* again, but they were too old and battered from the last Antarctic expedition. The best vessels to forge through the pack ice would be the Norwegian whalers like the *C. A. Larsen,* with their hulls of reinforced steel. Byrd couldn't afford such a ship. He took the next best, a strongly built wooden sailing vessel, the *Bear*. Like the *City,* she had heavy wooden sides and strong structural members along her keel. The *Bear* was longer, heavier, and faster and had the same ability to thrust upward against the force of ice, then bend and flex with the varied pressures.

She was an old ship that had already been tested in frozen waters. Obtained from a Scandinavian sealing company by Congress for the U.S. Navy in the late 1800s, the *Bear* served as the federal government's official presence off the Alaska coast, providing medical supplies, food, and law enforcement. After twenty-six years of service, she was retired to a museum in Oakland, California. The city sold her to Byrd for the nominal fee of a thousand dollars, in effect donating her to the expedition. The *Bear* survived the Antarctic and was eventually returned to the U.S. Navy during World War II; she patrolled the Greenland coast and was first to capture a German warship.

Byrd got hold of a second vessel, a steamship laid up since the end of World War I. He renamed it *Jacob Ruppert* in honor of one of the expedition's backers and loaded its four large cargo holds with expedition supplies.

───────◆───────

For nine months Victor and I spent most of our time soliciting the materials that we needed. Byrd supplied us with a number of contacts, and we developed quite a few of our own. I had learned through my experience with the dog food company that most large corporations are public-spirited — especially when their gifts receive public acknowledgment.

We did our first soliciting by letters, under Byrd's name, and he signed each one. The replies went directly to the admiral. If he received an affirmative answer, he would forward the letter to us. Victor and I would then write immediately and say, "As Admiral Byrd's supply officers, we welcome your letter and your questions. Here are the answers."

For instance, I would explain to one company that we wanted it to donate parkas. "We will have fifty-six men on this expedition. We must have clothing that can withstand temperatures as low as eighty degrees below zero." I'd tell another company that any goods we took had to be waterproofed. We tried to foresee all problems and to answer the questions as openly and fully as possible.

Sometimes I went in person because I loved presenting the expedition to corporation heads, telling them about Antarctica and asking for clothing, an airplane, electrical equipment, or whatever we specifically needed.

Byrd decided to take along as many planes as he could get. One manufacturer donated to the expedition a Curtiss-Condor transport with two engines of seven hundred fifty horsepower and a range of thirteen hundred miles. Byrd also received a single-engine Fokker, a Kellet autogiro, and a single-engine Pilgrim monoplane.

We picked up tractors, snowmobiles, and other vehicles, food and clothing, tools, rope, nails, telephones, radios, and an unbelievable amount of electrical equipment. We had to make our own tents and some specialized clothing. Two friends in New Hampshire, Ed Moody and Richard Moulton, both excellent drivers, were doing the work the three musketeers had done in 1927–1928, raising and training the dogs.

To this day, Ed Moody remains the very best sled maker. He has made sleds for sprint racing, long-distance racing, freight hauling, mountaineering, you name it. We once figured out that if placed end to end, these sleds would stretch from Boston to Chicago.

Like Ed, Dick Moulton still lives in New Hampshire and still owns, breeds, and drives sled dogs. Both men served with me in World War II in North Atlantic search-and-rescue operations, using dogsleds to traverse difficult terrain.

Bernt Balchen had agreed to be the chief pilot. Byrd arranged for a meteorologist to do weather reporting and investigating. Byrd and I both felt a keen sense of disappointment over Larry Gould's unavailability. In 1932 he had joined the faculty of Carleton College, Northfield, Minnesota, where he later became president. Antarctica and scientific research were always foremost in his mind, and he was affectionately called Mr. Antarctica.

During this period, Victor and I had close contact with Byrd. When he was in Boston, we usually saw him every day. Sometimes we talked on the telephone two or three times during business hours. Frequently Victor and I visited his house. The three of us took long walks on the esplanade behind it.

I liked those walks because Byrd was at his most informal. Often we functioned as his sounding board when he thought through a problem or considered a new possibility. It was a heady experience to be involved so closely in such a mammoth undertaking and with such a great man.

———————◆———————

For me, the most fascinating part of the 1934 expedition lay in Byrd's plan. The first part of the trip would be similar to that of the 1929–1930 expedition, establishing our living quarters. The difference lay in the winter period, from April to October. He planned for four people to live in a house at the foot of the Queen Maud Mountains, four hundred miles away from all the others. These four men would experience inland temperatures. They would know the joy and the terror of six months of utter isolation. Other than daily radio contact, the men would live alone and understand the privations and demands of a hostile land shrouded in total darkness.

"And, Norman," Byrd said, "of course I would like you to be one of the four men."

He spoke the magic words I longed to hear!

"No one in the world has ever done this before," Byrd said in a burst of enthusiasm. "Imagine what it will be like, living in the interior of the Antarctic continent. We shall prove that the human spirit can withstand every impediment." And he believed every word he spoke about his vision.

That was one of the things I liked about Byrd. He was a visionary—but one with both feet planted in practicality. He dreamed about the possibilities and wanted to do new things. Once he started dreaming, however, he paused long enough to figure out how to make the dream happen. This rare combination earned him respect from the world and the world's leaders.

Victor, Byrd, and I—depending largely on Victor's ingenuity—

worked out the difficulties in constructing a portable, prefabricated house. Especially in those days, it took a lot of planning. More than a decade would pass before most Americans began to hear about such buildings.

We carefully figured out the necessary amounts of food and equipment. Once we reached Antarctica, we would transport all of our equipment for the inland camp by plane. We knew the amount of available space and particularly the door design of the Curtiss-Condor. We calculated how to package materials to fit inside the plane for transport from the ship to a land base four hundred miles away.

This expedition would not depend quite as heavily on dogs, at least not for the transportation of our equipment. We would still need a number of them, however, for hauling supplies from shipside to Little America.

"And, Norman," Byrd repeated, "I would like you to be in charge of the dogs as well as live inland with us. We will take seven dogs with us for emergency evacuation."

How could I have refused an offer like that? Just thinking about being in Antarctica again gave me a renewed sense of energy. Throwing myself into the work, I felt like a new man. My depression lifted; only then did I realize how miserable I had been.

Iris noticed the difference in me after I agreed to help in the 1934 expedition. This change created a further barrier in our relationship. I think she felt guilty for not being able to go camping, drive dogs, shoot ducks or, as she said, make me happy. My wife excelled in domestic things, and her career was progressing nicely at N. W. Ayer and Son. I kept trying to explain, "Iris, our differences aren't your fault. I need a challenge, an adventure, something to do that I haven't done before."

She tried to understand. But the time and energy I threw into the expedition strained our relationship further. I easily forgot domestic problems once I reached the Boston naval yard each morning. The fast pace of making contacts and presentations swept me into the expedition, hardly allowing me time to think about Iris until the day was over. Working for the expedition was the beginning of the end for Iris and me; I think we both knew, but neither wanted to face the harsh reality.

Eventually we saw that our marriage could not work. We had both tried hard—Iris obviously more than I. Our differences were severe.

Deciding that both Jerry and Iris would be better off, I left. No child ought to be raised in an environment in which his parents hold such divergent views and whose personality differences cause countless arguments. Jerry was a year old when I moved away.

I understood then and realize even more today that the decision was completely selfish on my part. Yet it was as if I had no choice in the matter. Something inside made me follow the call of adventure.

During the next forty years I married two more times, and those marriages ended in divorce as well. I love women; I am just not a good husband. Or, as I have sometimes told myself as consolation, perhaps I had never found a woman during those years who understood that I could not conform to normal social patterns.

At the same time that the domestic situation was coming to an open and obvious conclusion, something was going on with Byrd that troubled me. I tried to ignore the inner voice for weeks, not wanting to think anything was amiss about Byrd or the expedition. I wanted to return to Antarctica more than I wanted anything else. Because of that desire, I refused to allow myself to believe what I knew was happening.

Decision Time

One spring morning, when the trees were dressing themselves in green, I accompanied Byrd on one of his walks along the esplanade. The soft winds across the Charles River Basin still carried the chill of winter, but we paid no attention.

The admiral had been talking about a particular problem he had dealt with the day before. He stopped speaking abruptly and lapsed into a lengthy silence. Being used to this habit of his, I walked beside him, knowing that he would speak up when he had decided how to say what he was thinking or had figured out the elusive solution.

"Norman," he said, and he kept his eyes straight ahead, "I've decided that we do not have time enough to establish a camp at the Queen Maud Mountains."

Not sure if he expected an answer from me, I said nothing. My mind was rapidly thinking about the equipment we had collected along with the things pledged but not yet received. As far as I could figure out, we had all the essentials and six more months before Byrd planned to leave. I couldn't understand why he should think we did not have sufficient time.

The silence lingered for a while, and I finally said, "I'm not sure I understand."

"I've had to revise my plans," Byrd said, "and won't be able to take you out there for the winter. I'm going to go out to the Queen Maud Mountains and spend the long night on the ice barrier alone."

Nothing he could have said would have shocked me more than those words. They struck me as forcefully as the time Byrd's maid told me I couldn't see the commander. She had shut the door on my plans for going to Antarctica. Now Byrd himself was slamming the door.

I didn't protest, however. Byrd worded his statement in a way that meant he had already decided. We were not having a conference; it was a *fait accompli*. Despite the heaviness of my heart, I managed to say the only thing I could think of: "I'm sorry to hear that."

He turned and looked at me. "You are going to be my second in command, in charge of Little America while I'm away."

He did not give me the chance to reject or accept this position, either. I'm convinced that he gave me the assignment to offset what he knew would be my great disappointment.

He explained what my position would entail, but I already knew the responsibility of the second in command. Ordinarily, such an offer would have elated me. But he was now saying that even though he wanted me on the expedition, I would remain at Little America — I'd stay back with the gang. Clever leader that he was, Byrd's statements squeezed me between feeling tremendously disappointed and highly honored by the offer of such a position.

We completed our walk shortly after that. I headed back to the office, terribly confused. Living under grave hardship, isolated at the foot of the Queen Maud Mountains, having opportunities for further exploration in the still-unknown land signified the greatest adventure I could imagine. I had been to Antarctica; I yearned to go back. But to have prepared myself for participation in one magnificent event and then to be told, "I have had to revise my plans," cut deeply.

I didn't believe his statement about not having enough time. Too confused to figure out his reasoning then, I still had enough sense to know that he had not been totally truthful.

Two days later the truth finally struck me. *Publicity.* By taking three of us with him, Byrd would have to divide the publicity among four. By staying alone, he would be the only man in the world who had endured such hardship. And he would be! I saw his decision as a grab for glory, to prove to the world once again that he was the first—and therefore the best.

A review of his public career made the reason seem obvious. He had always been first in all his great moments. Why should that change? Byrd had been the first to fly over the North Pole, the first to fly over the South Pole. He was the first to fly the Atlantic in a multiengine plane, arriving a few days after Lindbergh captured the world's attention with a single-engine. Now he would be the first to live alone and survive in total darkness, four hundred miles from the nearest human being.

This thirst for glory troubled me. Only then did I admit that Byrd had always been a publicity seeker. Either I had been too naive to see it, or perhaps the lionizing by the adoring public had molded such an attitude. He had gotten used to receiving the accolades and was seeking new ventures to capture the public's attention again. What better way than to brave the worst forces of nature on the world's coldest continent?

Emotions churned inside. The expedition was his, and no one else could have raised the money or excited the public. He had every right to choose whether to live alone or with others. I felt both hurt and depressed, but I never said those words to anyone. In fact, to everyone else who questioned me about the change of plans, I defended Byrd's right to do what he wanted about *his* expedition. I had no hold over him, not even for the original unsolicited promise of going into the interior with him.

But the news still hurt. And it hurt deeply.

In reviewing our conversations, I remembered that Byrd had never said, "I promise to take you." His words, when we first discussed the 1934 expedition, were, "I would like to have you go along."

For the next two days I felt so dejected that I didn't go in to the office. While my mind kept turning toward all the things that needed to be done for the expedition, I couldn't concentrate on my task and I couldn't exorcise my painful disappointment. "What should I do?" I asked aloud a hundred times. "Should I back out of the expedition? Go as second in command?"

My indecision couldn't go on indefinitely; I had to figure out a plan. Yet the more I turned things over in my mind, the more confused everything became. Worse, there was no one I could confide in, now that Iris and I were separated.

In desperation, I finally went to Father's house to talk to him. I had long recognized him as a very practical and sincere man. After my return from Antarctica, I felt closer to Father than ever before. We didn't talk differently or see more of each other. But giving me his watch had made me know how deeply he cared about me.

Father listened while I reviewed everything about the expedition, beginning with Byrd's initial contact and ending with what Byrd had said about revising his plans. Father had known the original plan about four of us living at the Queen Maud Mountains. He had remarked that it would be a valuable experience, one that would help me make a name for myself and perhaps lead to better job opportunities.

When I finished telling him the whole story, Father stared into space, choosing his words carefully. I knew whatever he said would come not only from his heart but also from his practical wisdom. "Norman, if you're not going out to the advance base with Byrd," he said, "you'll come back to America not having done anything new. You won't have climbed a mountain, you won't have done anything that anybody else couldn't accomplish if they had the chance to go to Little America."

I nodded, knowing he was right.

"You won't come back with any greater ability to earn a living. And, Norman, you can't go on exploring all your life; there's no money in that vocation. You've got to think seriously about your future and be practical."

I probably expected Father to say something like that, yet his words were not what I wanted to hear. Confused, I mentioned how much I wanted to return to the ice. Lamely, I said something about studying the penguins and learning more about life around Little America.

"Yes, you could," he said, "but that does not change what I've already said."

After a lengthy talk in which I mentioned every possibility for going under the new arrangement, Father concluded, "I don't see how you can avoid considering this latest development. Think it over carefully before you decide. I know you would go without the slightest hesitation if you could accompany Admiral Byrd out to the Queen Maud Mountains. But circumstances are now different. The revision of his plans places you at a juncture where you can change your mind."

Father's counsel forced me to come to a decision. I wanted to go with Byrd, even though I knew it was more practical to stay at home. The call of adventure was absolutely tremendous, like an addiction, filling my thoughts night and day. For months I had been living with the expectation of living in Antarctica again. Now it seemed as if everything was blowing up in my face.

I did not make the decision immediately — a bit unusual for me. I forced myself not to choose. Yet the choice was inevitable from the minute I walked out of Father's house. Another three weeks passed while I thought and rethought everything, determined to figure out how to overcome my disappointment. One day I would think that nothing was going to prevent my going, no matter how repetitive the experience. Then I would argue with myself, saying, You're only wasting your time if you go to Antarctica this way. You've been there once. It won't be as wonderful the second time anyway.

All the while, I was still working for Byrd. Three days after Byrd told me of his revised plans, I was back at the office, soliciting for equipment as energetically as ever. When I wrote or spoke, I found myself getting restimulated to go. Only in those moments alone did the conflict strike me.

Victor Czegka must have figured out something was wrong, but being the kind of friend he was, he didn't pry. He'd throw out a few hints that he knew all wasn't right, but he never came out and asked. And I didn't say anything.

At last, I was unable to put off the subject any longer. I had to talk to Victor about revising plans for Byrd's house.

"Victor, we need to talk about the expedition," I said. "We have to make changes."

He leaned back, waiting. I poured out the story of my walk with Byrd.

I had forgotten that one strange streak in Victor. When someone crossed him, he was like a wild man. Immediately his mind fastened on the months of work already put in. He had worked feverishly to develop the best yet simplest housing accommodation for four men. Victor had gone over every square foot of the house a dozen times, always trying to make it warmer and more practical. Most of all, once settled, Victor didn't like the idea of making one change.

He slammed his fist on the desk. "What the hell is this? Is he crazy?"

"I don't know," I said weakly.

"We have come up with a perfect building for four people. Now we have to cut it back so that it's suitable for just one man?"

"That's the Admiral's decision."

"Decision? Hell!" Victor yelled and swore, getting himself really stirred up. He moved around the small office, speaking loudly to me, going over everything he had already done. Even with his anger, he was also rethinking his plans for the house. "We design a stove for four, and now he's got to have a stove for just one man. I built a cabinet for four, and now I have to cut it down so that it provides for only one man. How am I going to do that in the time we have left? I've already had the lumber cut. These changes will delay everything. It'll cost more to cut everything down than to go ahead as we planned."

Victor continued, but I was no longer listening to his bitter words. I knew it didn't matter about the house — not to me, at least. In the end, Byrd kept the house exactly as Victor had planned it, without a single structural change. Byrd did not decrease the amount of food, clothing, or equipment. Everything went according to the original concept — except the number in the party.

Looking back, I realize that my decision to stay home involved more than Byrd's revised plans and my disappointment in his change. Father figured prominently. I didn't want to disappoint him again. He had stood aside when I dropped out of college to work with Grenfell. He had done nothing to prevent my going with Byrd in 1929. He had given me no argument when I said I wouldn't return to college. Each time he had stuck by me, and I knew he always would. Now I wanted to show my trust in him and his judgment. Father was, after all, a practical man, and he was trying to help me do what was best for my future.

In late August, a month before the departure of the expedition, the admiral and I met at his home. I was ready to face him. But he didn't make it easy for me. "Let's go for a walk," he said. I had wanted to talk to him at his desk, where I could concentrate on my words and not be distracted or interrupted by people we might meet. So many people recognized the admiral and always stopped to wish him well.

I stammered a bit before I found my words. "I have not decided *not* to go," I said, "but I no longer know whether it is *right* for me to go." Byrd was silent, so I continued. Without attribution, I repeated Father's arguments, then waited. A part of me was hoping he would counter all those arguments and persuade me to go back with him to the bottom of the world. But he was silent still.

A few days later I received the following letter from Byrd, dated August 29, 1933:

Dear Norman:

It is imperative from every angle that I consider your connection with the Expedition first and above all else from the standpoint of your future. We have reached a crisis in your life, and have a big decision to make, and my job is to encourage you to do the thing that will add most to the contents of your life. As to what decision will do that, no one but the good Lord can tell.

Apparently the three musketeers, you and Freddie and Eddie, have decided that it is very bad for you, from a business standpoint, to go again on an expedition with me. As to the accuracy of your conclusion, I do not know. It would not be for me to say anyhow. The only thing that I can do is to assume that you are correct. I am too deeply interested in your future to take the responsibility of disagreeing with you.

I would never forgive myself should I handicap you in your pursuit of success and happiness.

I cannot guarantee anything regarding the future. I have a terrific battle to collect enough of funds to leave. The expedition, therefore, may not leave the country. If we leave without funds I might not be able to pay you adequately. Even if we do, the expedition may not be a success and you may suffer thereby.

And on top of all that, if we do go, and you returned handicapped in business, as you think you will be, it seems to me that for your best good you had better accept one of the business offers you now have.

In saying this to you, I am not considering the expedition, which, of course, cannot replace you. I do not know just what we will do without you, but that is not the point.

My best to you always,

Faithfully yours,
R. E. Byrd

I continued to work for Byrd after I made my decision. I went to the office less and less, however, and allowed Victor and others to assume more responsibility. My heart was no longer in the expedition. I was going through a period of deep grief, although I wouldn't have been able to label my feelings by that name. I kept questioning my decision.

I drove to the Boston Navy Yard when Byrd sailed on September 25, 1933. We had a warm and friendly good-bye.

As he started up the gangplank he paused and smiled at me. We saluted each other. "Norman," he said in the softest tones he had ever used in talking to me, "I shall miss you." He turned and walked on board.

A month after Byrd sailed on the cutter, *Bear,* the *Jacob Ruppert* left from Newport News, Virginia. Between the two ships they carried fifty-six men who would stay at Little America, plus the volunteer ships' crews, altogether numbering seventy-two. On this expedition they took one hundred fifty-three dogs.

On January 17, 1934, the *Bear* moved into the Bay of Whales. Even with the accumulation of three years of snow, Little America had remained virtually intact. Surprisingly, the field telephone that connected the main buildings functioned fine. The crew found quantities of food and equipment perfectly preserved.

Byrd revised his plan once more about going four hundred miles into the interior. For his own reasons, he had the house erected only two hundred miles inland, at a point midway between the Queen Maud Mountains and Little America. There, at Advance Base, he would live alone for one hundred and eighty days.

Bad weather delayed unloading the ships and sending out an advance party. On February 26, 1934, the *Bear,* at last fully unloaded, headed back for New Zealand. When the carpenters started inland, they found it bitterly cold — far worse than it had been in 1929. The temperature hovered at sixty degrees below zero.

On March 22, 1934, Byrd climbed into his Pilgrim monoplane, and Balchen flew him to Advance Base. There the work party had nearly finished the house. They had first dug a great hole in the snow and fitted the prefab hut into it. Two supply tunnels leading from the hut had been stocked with food and equipment. Following Victor's plans, workers had constructed the tunnels deep enough so that Byrd could walk erect and enter directly from the hut without going outside.

Six days later, March 28, 1934, the construction crew, who had come across the ice with tractors, said good-bye to Byrd. In convoy style the men pulled out and headed back for Little America.

One of the most delightful stories of the 1934 expedition has never been published before. Ike Schlossback, its principal, related it to me after he returned.

More adventurous than intelligent, Ike constantly tried to figure out ways to make himself a fortune. Years earlier he had lost an eye in a Navy air crash. His disability pension and his small farm-turned-into-an-airstrip kept him going, but he dreamed of making big money. Although he never ended up rich, he filled his life with one scheme or strange idea after another.

Unfortunately, Ike's best and most ambitious idea, conceived in secrecy and carried out entirely alone, never provided him with just recognition.

The tale began in April 1934. Byrd was ready to depart from Little America for his solitary, pioneering winter stay in the Antarctic interior, his goal being to provide invaluable information about weather conditions as well as to test the limits of his own endurance. The expeditionary crew lined up in the mess hall to say good-bye.

As each man approached, Byrd ritually shook hands and said good-bye, making applicable personal remarks. The line grew shorter as each man expressed hope for the admiral's safety and well-being before walking away.

Ike, an old Navy friend of Byrd's, intentionally took his place at the end of the line. "Good luck, Admiral."

"I feel confident that all will go well at Little America," Byrd said, "because you'll be here, Ike."

"Thanks, Admiral," Ike replied, having carefully prepared his next statement. "But there's one thing I'd like to ask you. That is, if you don't mind, sir?" A quick turning of his head assured Ike that no one else was close enough to hear.

"Not at all."

"It's about the Fairchild left from your first expedition. I wanted to ask a favor."

"The Fairchild?" A puzzled expression clouded the admiral's face. "We not only abandoned the plane but by now at least ten feet of packed snow and ice must cover it."

"I know that, sir," Ike said quickly. "That's the point. The plane's still up there on the hill someplace, unmarked and snow covered. From everything I've heard, Balchen left the plane in top condition. If I can find the Fairchild while you're gone — *if I can find it* — will you take the plane back to New Jersey for me?"

"Even if you located the plane, you'd have difficulty in digging —"

"I've already figured out how to do that. But you see, sir, *if* I can find the Fairchild, I'd like to use it back in New Jersey. You know, advertise the plane as having been involved in Admiral Richard Byrd's two great expeditions to the South Pole. I'd fly people at five dollars a ride on

Sundays. The plane'd help me make a living for a long while."

Byrd, always a soft touch for his men and especially for a former shipmate, said unhesitatingly, "Yes, of course, Ike."

"Thank you, Admiral, sir," Ike responded, snapping to attention and saluting. "And good luck. I'll see you in the spring."

Ike, taking advantage of his reputation as a loner, had started his hunt the day the crew arrived at Little America months earlier. Bernt Balchen had given him fairly specific directions on where to look for the Fairchild. Sneaking away from camp at various times, often when the others were sleeping, Ike persisted in his search. Six days before Byrd's departure he had located the Fairchild. Now, with Byrd's permission, Ike was ready for action.

Ike never told another person of his discovery and had no intentions of sharing his money-making scheme with anyone. The long night was coming, Ike had no responsibilities, and he figured on spending those months digging out the airplane.

Each morning after breakfast Ike disappeared, staying away for ten hours before sauntering back into camp a few minutes before supper. When questioned about his activity, he would say vaguely, "Oh, I've been trying to locate some equipment left over from 1929. They discarded all sorts of things, and I know they're still here somewhere." Soon none of the crew paid any attention to Ike's comings and goings. Most men just thought he was strange.

Within a month the sunlight totally disappeared, but the loner faithfully went out every day in his so-called search. When others, bored with staying at camp, offered to help, Ike discouraged them without actually refusing. If a volunteer persisted, Ike agreed, walking with the man to some spot beyond the Fairchild.

"Take this," Ike would say as he shoved a metal pole into the helper's hand. Ike would carefully explain his method. "Every five feet, you poke and probe—but you have to push this pole hard—just as far into the ice as you can. If you don't touch anything solid, move a few more feet and try again."

The helper, dressed in his warmest clothes with face mask and fur mittens and using only a flashlight, would begin probing, expecting to find something. But it was never long before the volunteer returned to the warmth of the mess hall, muttering all the way back about crazy Ike.

After half a dozen men had gone out with Ike on his search and found nothing, the volunteering stopped; instead, the crew spent much of their idle time joking about Schlossback's strange and relentless hunt.

Meanwhile, under ten feet of crusted snow, Ike was systematically and painstakingly tunneling around the abandoned plane—all of this under the snow with only a dim lantern borrowed from the dog drivers. Ike told me that five shovelfuls filled a tiny sled, which he then pulled to the surface and emptied downwind. Usually the wind carried most of the snow away, but when a buildup occurred, Ike felt little concern. The next high wind would level the dumped snow to the barrier surface.

The hardest work involved shoveling on the inside of the plane. In the years since the plane had been abandoned, high winds had driven snow through the tiniest openings, tightly packing it inside.

After weeks of boring labor, Ike finally freed the plane's interior and engine cowlings. Everything seemed stiff but workable. A pleased Ike realized that with only a few adjustments, the plane would be in flying condition again. He took out the magneto and carburetor and replaced minor parts from the machine stores at Little America. No one in the stores paid any attention as Ike appropriated what he needed.

During these weeks of digging, no crew member suspected Ike's secret. In fact, Ike became the subject of increasing ridicule because of his seemingly impossible task and his unflagging zeal. He took the joking well, allowing the men to think what they wanted. In his mind, he imagined what they would say when, after the admiral's return, they saw the Fairchild ready to load onto the ship.

On blizzardy days, Ike remained in camp, mixing with the crew, still telling no one of his find. He could have worked on his task because by then the plane was protected inside the cave he had dug around it. But if he had stayed out during a blizzard, the others might have become suspicious.

When spring approached, Ike secretly took gasoline, five gallons at a time, out to the Fairchild. Once the tanks were topped, he had more shoveling ahead to get the plane out of the tunnel. Fortunately, the plane pointed downhill. He had to evacuate all the snow in front of the plane except for a two-foot protective wall. Ike dug, clearing a distance of forty feet from wing tip to wing tip and another twelve feet from the skis on the bottom of the plane to the top. No little task for one man! But Ike, filled with his dreams, stayed at it.

By early October, when the sun returned, Ike had completed the major digging, needing only to knock down the front wall and to start the engine. The pilot had mentally run these last two operations over and over so there would be no hitch on the final day.

In the meantime, Byrd had been radioing ominous reports to Little America. He finally admitted he was sick and getting weaker. For days at a time, he didn't keep radio schedules. All became concerned.

Second-in-command John Poulter finally decided to send the big Fokker, brought specifically on the 1934 expedition to bring the admiral back. As backups he planned to dispatch dog teams and over-the-snow vehicles. Poulter chose the day when he was assured that the plane could land in daylight and return to Little America before dark; he would have only an hour of light to spare.

With this change in Byrd's arrangements, a plan formed in Ike's mind. He decided to follow the rescue plane and let the admiral see that he had located and reactivated the Fairchild. Ike reasoned that his flight would also show Byrd how much he appreciated the promised gift, and that the demonstration would help lift Byrd's spirits.

At the camp everyone cooperated to make the rescue a success. Ike helped mechanics with inconsequential tasks just to show his good spirits, but he still disappeared as often as he could. Even the cook, George Tennant, prepared hot chicken bouillon to go along, figuring the soup would be a welcome treat for the admiral's sick body, although at the time no one knew what ailed Byrd.

On the big day the crew hurried through breakfast, everyone alert and eager for the event. Ike sat silently drinking another cup of coffee while the men filed out and forgot him. Poulter had scheduled takeoff for eleven o'clock, with dog teams and snowmobiles leaving two hours earlier. Unnoticed, Ike slipped out of Little America and raced over to his hideaway. He furiously broke down the wall.

187

At ten o'clock the pilots reported to Poulter, "We'll have a twenty-minute delay," and explained the need for a rather insignificant repair. A disgusted Poulter immediately postponed the plane mission for twenty-four hours with the comment, "You've had all winter to get that plane ready and you've failed by twenty minutes."

The mild criticism spread around camp, leaving everyone on edge. Several of the men grumbled, concerned that the delay would only make Byrd's condition worse. No one dared say that directly to Poulter.

Ike, working feverishly, had broken the wall down long before eleven o'clock. He had not been in camp to hear of the delay, and he was too busy to listen for the big plane's engines. The unauthorized pilot concentrated on last-minute preparation of his plane. After all his work, he wondered, would the Fairchild start?

He had the engine heater going for a full hour. The crankcase oil was warmed on a converted blowtorch. Everything seemed ready. Fortunately, a calm wind prevailed; the temperature was twenty-five degrees below zero.

Then came Ike's crucial moment—after a whole winter's labor. The starter button rotated the propeller. There was a backfire and then the familiar sound of the whirring prop. After adjusting the mixture control, Ike turned on the lights, ready to taxi. Although the oil pressure indicator remained on the low part of the dial, Ike wanted out, and he gunned the engine. The skis, resting on poles to lessen the starting friction, moved, and the plane came out of its four-year entombment. Faster and faster Ike gunned the engine until finally one ski lifted, followed by the other. The Fairchild was airborne.

The lights and noise startled the others at camp. Everyone dashed outside, confused and excited. After a slow, long turn, the Fairchild steadied at one thousand feet, and Ike made five circles around the camp, each turn a little tighter. Shipmates, stunned at what they were seeing, waved and cheered him on—all except Poulter and the jealous pilots. On the fifth time around, the Fairchild gained speed in a low buzz over the camp and headed south.

Poulter alerted the admiral by radio, first about the postponement and then about Ike.

As Ike flew off he realized that the other plane had not gone. Not having a radio, Ike assumed that complications had postponed its takeoff or that it might not be able to take off at all. That's when a new plan formed in Ike's fertile brain. He would have the supreme honor of rescuing Byrd and in the hazardous rescue show the admiral how deeply he appreciated the promise of the Fairchild.

An hour later Ike spotted the base and dropped a smoking red flare. The smoke from the flare indicated the wind direction, enabling Ike to land.

As Ike moved in for the landing, he saw a lone figure standing at the tunnel entrance, wildly waving his arms. After taxiing toward Byrd, Ike opened the side window and cut the engine. He called out, "Hello, Admiral!"

Byrd now stood with his hands on his hips, legs spread apart. From the portion of his face that showed, anyone could see that the man was very ill, and very angry besides. Anyone but Ike, that is.

"Ike, what the hell are you doing here?"

"Why, I came to rescue you, Admiral. I got the plane going—"

"Shut your window. Go back to Little America!"

"But I'm here to—"

"Get out of here! I'll be rescued by my own crew."

A confused Ike responded in the only way he knew how. "Aye, aye, sir," Ike said and restarted the engine for his return to Little America.

Ike never did understand Byrd's puzzling behavior. "A rescue is a rescue," he told me. "What difference does it make how it's done?"

I had long learned that Byrd's quixotic behavior formed part of the great man's personality. And, as sick as he was, Byrd was determined to have *his* plans carried out.

———————◆———————

Most people in America later heard that Byrd had almost died in the hut. Byrd had a small, round stove that was vented through a length of stovepipe to the outside. Making the system work properly caused the admiral no end of problems. Blowing snow often filled the outside vent, which forced him to remove it and melt out the packed snow on the stove before replacing the pipe. At first he thought the vent was the only problem, when all the while the house was filling with gas fumes leaking directly from the stove because of incomplete combustion.

Byrd couldn't discover how fumes were accumulating in the hut even when the vent was clear, and he tried shutting down the stove for hours at a time, leaving the door slightly ajar. That worked well enough until the weather worsened. On May 20 he recorded a low temperature of minus seventy-four. Unable to bear the cold, Byrd closed the door and started the stove. Within an hour, dangerous fumes filled the room.

By the end of May, the fumes had become so concentrated that carbon monoxide poison almost killed him. For several days Byrd broke radio contact; the men at Little America worried about the silence, and no one knew what, if anything, they should do. Having no orders, they waited. And prayed. And hoped.

Byrd stayed alone in Advance Base for one hundred and thirty days. By his own admission, he was sick for seventy-two of those days. During the worst times, he wrote deathbed letters to his wife, Marie, his son, Richard, Jr., and his two daughters, Emily and Catherine.

Finally, when the men at Little America had agreed that Byrd must be sick or possibly dead, the rescue mission was readied. By the time the official rescue party arrived to pick him up, Byrd was so sick that he could not travel. He stayed another sixty-four days before he felt he was strong enough to survive an overland journey should the rescue plane be forced to land.

Although he had been angry with Ike Schlossback, Byrd never mentioned the incident again, behaving as if it hadn't happened. And the admiral lived up to his promise to Ike: He brought the Fairchild back to the States, and Ike did charge people for rides.

Two years later Ike was submarine commander of wealthy Lincoln Ellsworth's attempted expedition to the North Pole. The crew planned to bore a hole through the ice from below. Delays ultimately forced them to abandon the expedition.

On the westward journey across the Atlantic and before reaching the continental shelf, Ike Schlossback, ever the maverick skipper, put the submarine into an outside loop—turning the ship in a complete circle under water. The movement threw people against the bulkheads and injured several crew members. Battery acid sprayed and spilled. Dishes broke. The angry crew, ready to mutiny, reported a wide variety of minor damage.

Although not recorded in history books, Ike's crazy feat was the only time a submarine had ever been put into an outside loop.

Epilogue

For months after turning Byrd down, I tortured myself by asking, "Have I made a mistake? Should I have gone?" Being second in command would have been both an honorable and a responsible position. I might have used that title and experience as an item in my résumé for future positions. But even though I didn't go, my thoughts followed every step of progress reported through the newspapers and radio.

Finally, the time came for me to get on with the rest of my life. I reentered business, working for the N. W. Ayer company again and then moving on to other jobs. World War II came, and I found great adventure during those days. I also served during the Korean conflict.

Byrd never held a grudge against me for not going on the 1934 expedition. I always knew that. His letter said clearly how he felt. If I ever doubted his friendship and loyalty, he proved both to me a decade later.

During World War II, Byrd telephoned me from Washington, D.C. "Where are you stationed?" The interest was typical of his generous way of looking after "his" men.

"I'm stationed at Goose Bay, Labrador," I said. "Right now I'm at Presque Isle, Maine, on temporary duty."

"And what's your rank?"

"Captain."

"How long have you been a captain?"

By then I had held the rank for six months, and I told him so.

"Norman, we're in for a long war. We need more good men like you in leadership. You ought to be a colonel by now."

"Well, I'm not," I said and laughed.

"You will be," he said. He hung up a few minutes later.

On his own the admiral contacted his brother, Harry Byrd, the senior senator from Virginia, who then took the matter to the Pentagon. Within weeks I received a promotion to major. Eventually I attained the rank of lieutenant colonel without help from Byrd.

Over the years Byrd and I had few contacts. Every Christmas he sent a gift and a card or letter. The one I most prize was written December 18, 1952:

Dear Norman:

When I sat on the hunk of ice at the bottom of the world for six months of the winter night alone in the dark shadow of the Pole I had a perfect opportunity to assess my values.

And my conclusion in the end was that the most important things to a man are his family and friends.

And now eighteen years later, as I am traveling down the other side of the mountain, I have not only verified the conclusion drawn at Advance Base but have found that my old friends, whether I see them or not, become more valuable to me year by year.

And you know, you are one of those friends; and the privilege the Yuletide gives us is to say such things.

And so, with the basket of apples which I, as of old, am sending you for Christmas go fervent wishes for you and yours that all

the many things that go to make up your life will be as you would
have them, so that the years ahead will bring peace and happiness.

Your friend,

Dick

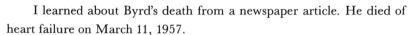

I learned about Byrd's death from a newspaper article. He died of
heart failure on March 11, 1957.

Only a few weeks earlier I had seen the admiral in his dress uniform
at Arlington National Cemetery, accompanying the widow of Carl Petersen, one of our Little America radio operators. At the open grave, Byrd
beautifully expressed feelings of loyalty for one of his shipmates. I knew
he would have made the same warm comments had it been my funeral.

I wanted to attend Byrd's funeral, so I contacted a friend, Commander Bill Scheibel of the U.S. Coast Guard. By then I had resigned
from the Air Force and was without the privilege of free transportation.
Scheibel arranged for a hop on a night flight from Bolling Field, near
Washington, D.C. From there I went by bus to Arlington.

At the graveside, I looked around, surprised and saddened to discover that I was the only member of the first expedition who had been
able to get to the funeral.

Although Byrd and I had not been intimate friends, that indivisible
bond between us had remained. Having friends among the famous and
celebrated can open doors and offer certain privileges. I never made use
of the privilege, yet in Admiral Richard E. Byrd I knew I had a friend I
could call upon at any time or for any need.

Byrd's funeral was spectacular, with many VIPs in attendance. A
horse-drawn caisson always gives me shivers of pride. The taps blown at
the graveside brought tears to my eyes. I made no attempt to wipe them
away, and I didn't care if anyone else noticed. I was saying good-bye to a
great man.

I stood at attention, listening to taps while vivid memories flashed
through my mind. I thought of my first meeting with Byrd at Wonalancet, when he inspected the dogs . . . my carrying him by sled to Little

America . . . our walks along the barrier in Antarctica . . . his phone calls and letters . . . his parting words when he left for his second expedition, back to Antarctica . . . In my mind I saw him again on the frozen continent as we hastened to board the battered *City* in the Bay of Whales after our year at the bottom of the world.

"It's over, Norman," he had said. The smile — I saw the smile again, too. "We did it."

Yes, I thought. *We did it.*

Norman Vaughan, 1989.

Norman Vaughan, a mushing legend, competes in the Iditarod sled dog race across Alaska every year and has finished five times since he turned 70, most recently in 1990 at age 85. He has crashed a presidential inaugural with a dog team, mushed dogs with the Pope, and driven a snowmobile from Alaska to Boston, among other exciting accomplishments. He lives in Trapper Creek, Alaska, with his wife, Carolyn Muegge Vaughan.